PEARSON
PUBLISHING

Student Handbook for
Information Technology

for KS3, KS4 and GCSE

Gareth Williams

Illustrations by Matthew Foster-Smith

Name...

Address ....

....

....

Date of exams: (1) ....

(2) ....

Coursework deadline dates: (1) ....

(2) ....

Exam board ....

Syllabus number..

Candidate number ....

Centre number...

Further copies of this publication may be obtained from:

Pearson Publishing
Chesterton Mill, French's Road, Cambridge CB4 3NP
Tel 01223 350555   Fax 01223 356484
Email info@pearson.co.uk   Web site http://www.pearson.co.uk/education/

ISBN: 1 85749 534 9

Published by Pearson Publishing 1997
© Pearson Publishing 1997

Revised 1997
Reprinted six times 1997
Reprinted four times 1998
Second edition 1998
Reprinted 1998
Reprinted 1999

Contents

Introduction

This book has been written for students learning about Information Technology in secondary schools. It provides a comprehensive background to go with the practical skills which are learnt at Key Stages 3 and 4. The book contains both the material required by the National Curriculum and the syllabus content for the London, MEG, SEG and NEAB examination boards for GCSE IT courses and IT short courses.

The world of Information Technology and computing is changing at such a speed that no textbook will remain up-to-date for more than a couple of years. This book is based on the latest developments relevant for 1998 and 1999, including reference to Pentium 2 processors, while meeting the examination board requirements for 1999/2000.

Information Technology is an exciting subject and understanding the theory as well as the practical skills will benefit all students.

Using this book

Remember that this is your book, so you may decide to personalise it, make notes in the margin, use the checklist in the contents to assess your progress, etc.

The index at the back of the book will help you to find specific topics.

Answers to the questions are provided on pages 116 to 117.

Feedback

If you have any comments or suggestions as to how this book may be improved, please send them to the author via Pearson Publishing.

1 Types of computer

Computers can be divided into five types:

- supercomputers
- mainframe computers
- minicomputers
- embedded computers
- microcomputers.

Supercomputers

Supercomputers are the fastest and the most expensive computers. They have huge processing power and are used mainly for scientific and engineering applications. This power makes them suitable for applications such as weather forecasting and complex graphical techniques. Supercomputers cost many millions of pounds. An example of a supercomputer is the CRAY YM/P.

Mainframe computers

Mainframes are used in large companies for data processing and by scientists for complex mathematical calculations. They have also found a new role as network servers on the Internet. On average a mainframe would cost £4m and an example of a mainframe is IBM's System/390.

Minicomputers

Minicomputers are used by smaller businesses to manage their data processing needs. Complex programs like relational databases run efficiently on these computers and older database programs can be linked to newer programs running on the Internet. An example of a minicomputer is IBM's AS/400.

Embedded computers

From telephones to missiles, and from cameras to washing machines, these modern devices contain built-in computers or embedded systems. There is no need for these systems to use keyboards and computer monitors since the inputs required come from the device's sensors, and outputs control the operation of the device.

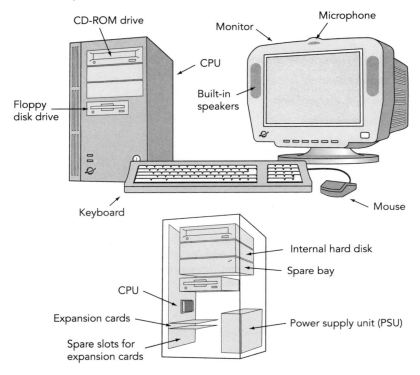

A modern PC microcomputer with cutaway showing internal features

Microcomputers are now in wide use in homes, schools and businesses. Microcomputers together with CD-ROM drives, stereo sound and software are available for under £1000. Notebooks are portable microcomputers approximately 30 cm across, 20 cm back and 3 cm thick.

The screen is on the inside of the top flap which hinges open. The keyboard is more compact but has the same layout of keys as the larger desktop microcomputer; they are also as powerful with Pentium processors, high capacity hard drives and CD-ROM drives.

Although notebooks have the advantage over desktop microcomputers in size, weight and portability they are slightly more expensive and will not allow standard interface cards to be slotted in.

2 Structure of a computer

The diagram below shows a simple structure for the operation of a computer. Data is obtained for processing by the computer and then the results of the processing are output from the system:

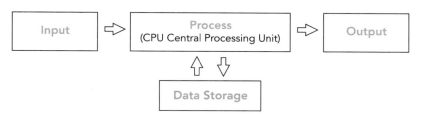

Input

The need to capture data quickly and accurately has led to a wide range of input devices. Some of these input devices make use of human touch, light, magnetism, sound and control sensors. Each type of input device has been designed for a specific purpose.

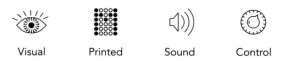

| Touch | Light | Magnetism | Sound | Control |

Process

In home, business and school microcomputers, a main processing chip called the CPU (central processing unit) handles the instructions from the computer program and processes the data. In larger computers several processing chips will be used.

Output

The results of processing are passed to output devices. The most common output devices are the computer monitor and the printer. Output devices are considered in Chapter 4.

| Visual | Printed | Sound | Control |

3 Input devices

Keyboard

The most common way of entering data into a computer is through the keyboard. The layout of the letters on the keyboard is standard across many countries in the world and is called a QWERTY keyboard. These are the first few characters on the top row of letters. Keyboards are easy to use, particularly by touch typists who can type without looking at the keyboard.

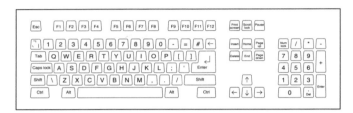

A QWERTY keyboard

Concept keyboard

A concept keyboard consists of a flatbed of contact switches covered by a flexible membrane. Programmers can allocate one or more switches to respond in different ways. Overlays with pictures and symbols are placed over the membrane. Uses of the concept keyboard include primary schools where the overlays are designed with interesting picture layouts. Children press on particular symbols or pictures in response to the activity being done. These keyboards are very flexible: an overlay for a five-year-old can be designed quite differently to an overlay for a ten-year-old which would be more detailed.

Concept keyboards are also used in restaurants where the checkout tills use symbols to speed up the data entry. They can also be used in hostile environments, for example on North Sea oil platforms where the keyboard allows workers to use computer controlled machinery through the keyboard without it being damaged by the salt spray or chemicals on the platform.

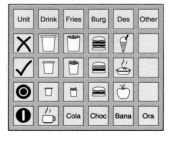

Mouse

 The movement of the mouse by the user's hand is mirrored by the pointer on the monitor screen. Under the mouse is a ball which rolls as the mouse is moved. This movement of the ball causes two shafts to rotate inside the mouse, one shaft records the movement in the north-south direction and the other shaft records the east-west movement. When the screen pointer is over an icon or menu selection the mouse button can be clicked, double clicked or dragged (moved with the button held down) to activate a process.

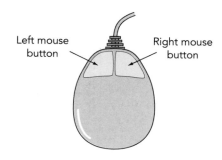

Left mouse button

Right mouse button

Graphics tablet

 The graphics tablet is a flat pad which the user can write on, or draw on, with a device similar to a pen called a stylus. The surface of the pad is sensitive to the position of the stylus and the stylus itself is sensitive to the pressure applied by the user. As the stylus is moved across the pad, the movement is translated to a drawing on the computer monitor. The harder the user presses on the stylus, the thicker the line drawn on the screen. A typical resolution (see page 13) for a graphics tablet used in art work and computer aided design (CAD) is $^1/_{250}$ cm.

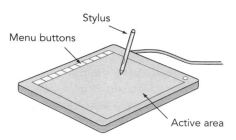

Stylus

Menu buttons

Active area

Touch-screen

 On touch-sensitive screens there are criss-crossing beams of infra-red light just in front of the glass on the computer monitor. When a user touches the glass with their finger, two sets of rays are blocked: the rays travelling from side to side (y co-ordinates) and the rays going from top to bottom (x co-ordinates). The computer can detect the position of the finger from the light sensors placed on the opposite side of the monitor screen to the light sources, and respond accordingly (see diagram overleaf). Touch-screens are easy to use (user friendly) and might be found as input devices in public places (eg museums) with information software.

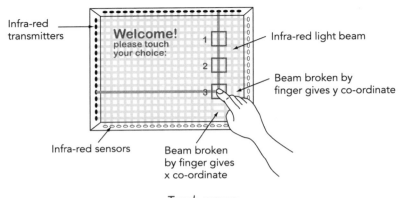

Infra-red transmitters

Welcome!
please touch
your choice:

1
2
3

Infra-red light beam

Beam broken by
finger gives y co-ordinate

Infra-red sensors

Beam broken
by finger gives
x co-ordinate

Touch-screen

Scanners

Scanners enable both pictures and text to be input to a computer. Scanning text in order to recognise the words and letters requires special software and this is covered on the next page under OCR. The most common type of scanner is the flat-bed but smaller and cheaper hand-held scanners which are rolled over the document/picture are also available. On the flat-bed scanner the picture being scanned is placed face down on a glass plate like a photocopier. A bright light is slowly moved across the picture and the reflected light is focused onto a bank of light sensors using mirrors and lenses. White reflects the most light and black reflects the least. For each tiny part of the picture the strength of the reflection is captured and converted into a digital signal for input to the computer. Scanned pictures which can be manipulated using sophisticated image editing software are often used in publishing work.

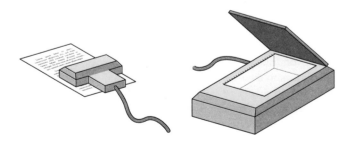

Hand-held scanner   *Flat-bed scanner*

Optical character recognition (OCR)

Scanning devices are also used to recognise letters, numbers and words. The ability to scan the characters accurately depends on how clear the writing is. Scanners have improved to be able to read different styles and sizes of type and also neat handwriting.

One application of optical character recognition is reading postcodes on letters at sorting offices so that letters can be sorted automatically.

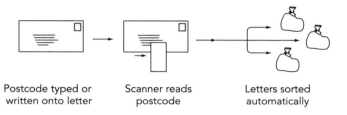

| Postcode typed or | Scanner reads | Letters sorted |
| written onto letter | postcode | automatically |

Optical mark reader (OMR)

Optical mark readers detect marks made on paper. It is usually recommended that the marks are made with a soft (HB) pencil. The reader scans across the paper with an infra-red light. Where there is no mark, there is a strong reflection of light off the white paper; where a mark has been made, the reflection is reduced.

This form of input is often used for student answers to multiple-choice examination papers and for choosing the numbers on lottery tickets.

BOARD A			£1	
1	▌	3	4	5
6	7	8	9	10
11	12	13	▌	15
16	▌	18	19	20
21	22	23	▌	25
26	▌	28	29	30
31	32	33	34	35
36	37	38	▌	40

Bar code reader

Bar codes are made up of black and white stripes of different thicknesses. These lines represent numbers and are read with a wand or laser scanner. They are now used on almost all goods sold in shops and supermarkets and provide a fast and reliable method of entering data even when the surfaces being read are curved.

The numbers of the bar code hold coded information about the product, including the country of manufacture, the name of the manufacturer, a product item code and a check digit. They do not hold information directly for the name, description or price of the product. When the

numbers on the bar code are scanned the data is passed to the computer which then returns information about the product.

Digital camera

The picture taken with a digital camera is stored in computer memory rather than on film as in an ordinary camera.

The different colours that make up the picture are converted to digital signals (codes of '0s' and '1s') by sensors placed behind the lens. These pictures can then be displayed directly onto the computer monitor or imported into a graphics/art package for editing.

Light from the image passes through the lens to a sensor inside the camera

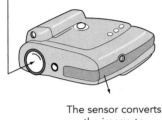

The sensor converts the image to digital data

The image can now be stored on floppy disk or loaded into a computer

Video digitiser

The video digitiser enables video signals from a standard camcorder to be displayed in a window on the computer screen. Video sequences can be stored on the hard disk of the computer and used in other computer programs. Still images can also be captured; the video digitiser allows the user to select the best image from the sequence.

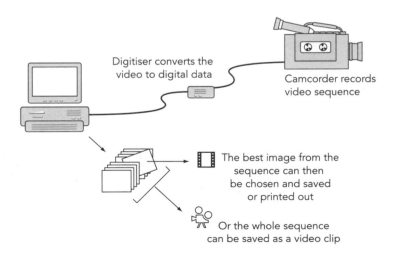

Digitiser converts the video to digital data

Camcorder records video sequence

The best image from the sequence can then be chosen and saved or printed out

Or the whole sequence can be saved as a video clip

Magnetic ink character recognition (MICR)

This method of inputting data into a computer is used on bank cheques. The numbers printed at the bottom of a cheque have magnetic particles in the ink. These can be read very quickly by machines (as many as 3000 cheques per minute). Three numbers are printed on a cheque: the cheque number (each cheque in the cheque book has its own number); the bank or building society's sort code; and the customer's account number.

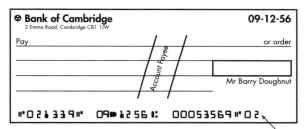

Characters written in magnetic ink

When a cheque is written and presented to the bank, a fourth number is added using the special magnetic ink which can be read by the computer. This last number to be typed on the cheque by the bank is the amount the cheque is made out for. MICR is very reliable as a means of entering data into a computer because it can still be read even if someone scribbles over the numbers with a pen.

Magnetic stripes

Magnetic stripes are thin strips of magnetic tape, often found on the back of plastic credit and debit cards. When the card is used the stripe passes record and playback heads, similar to a tape recorder, which reads data from, and writes data to, the stripe.

Cards with stripes are used, for example, to withdraw cash from the cash dispenser machines (called Automatic Teller Machines or ATMs) on the walls of banks, building societies and shopping centres.

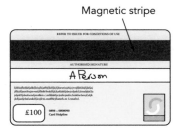

Magnetic stripe

9

Speech or voice input

 Speech or voice input is a rapidly developing means of input to a computer. It is already an important method for people who are severely handicapped, or where the user's hands need to be free to do other things, but it requires fast processing and large amounts of memory. Programs are available which will recognise continuous speech input, translating the words directly into a word processor. Some words sound the same but are used in different contexts, eg 'weather' and 'whether' or 'sail' and 'sale'. These programs can select the appropriate spelling from the sentence that is spoken.

Computer translates speech to text

Microphone

Musical Instrument Digital Interface (MIDI)

 MIDI was developed as a standard for linking musical keyboards together. Computers fitted with MIDI interface boards can be connected to MIDI instruments allowing the music being played to be stored and displayed by the computer on the monitor. The computer can display the music as a musical score and notes can be added, altered or deleted. The music being played can also be printed out from the computer.

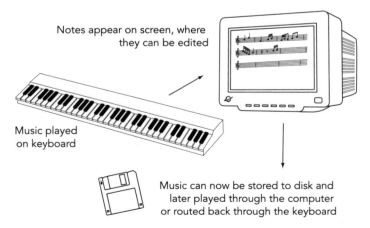

Notes appear on screen, where they can be edited

Music played on keyboard

Music can now be stored to disk and later played through the computer or routed back through the keyboard

Control devices

There are many different input devices associated with controlling machinery and monitoring and logging the environment. Three of the simplest and most common devices are switches, and light and heat sensors. There are also sensors for pressure, stress and strain in materials, air pressure, humidity, pH sensors to measure acidity, etc.

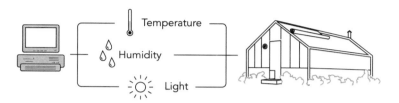

Greenhouse control

Switches

When computer input comes from mechanical devices like automated machinery in factories, switches can be used. Mechanical switches such as slide, toggle and push buttons can be used, activated by the operator or moving equipment.

Magnetic switches are activated when a magnet comes close to the switch. The two contacts which form the switch come into contact in the magnetic field.

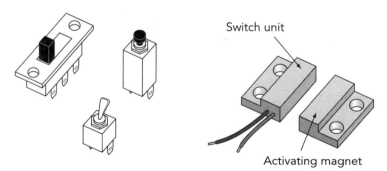

Some mechanical switches   *A magnetic switch*

Thermistors

Thermistors are electronic devices that can be used to measure temperature since their resistance changes with temperature. Using this device, the computer can input the temperature and respond accordingly, perhaps by switching on or off other circuits controlling heaters.

Thermistor

Light-dependent resistors (LDRs)

Light-dependent resistors are light sensors that change their electrical resistance according to the amount of light falling on them. The brighter the light, the lower the resistance. These, together with heat sensors, could be used in a computer automated greenhouse to maintain the ideal growing conditions for the plants.

Light-sensitive surface

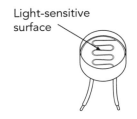

Light-dependent resistor

Questions

1   Name two input devices that might be used with a desktop publishing package in addition to the mouse, keyboard and disk drive.

   ....

   ....

2   The bar code on a tin of beans contains which of the following pieces of information?

   ☐ Sell-by date   ☐ Country of origin

   ☐ Shop name   ☐ The size of the tin

3   Why are price details not part of the bar code?

   ....

   ....

4   Name an input device that could be used:

   a   to control conditions in an automated greenhouse ....

   b   by young children in a primary school ....

   c   to read the postcode on a letter ....

   d   to mark a student's multiple-choice answer paper ....

   e   to obtain money from a cash dispenser machine ....

4 *Output devices*

Monitors

The computer monitor, screen or VDU (visual display unit) is the most common output device. A popular size for monitor screens is 15 inches. The size is always measured diagonally, from corner to corner. Larger monitors make working at a computer easier on the eyes and are essential for use in desktop publishing and design work.

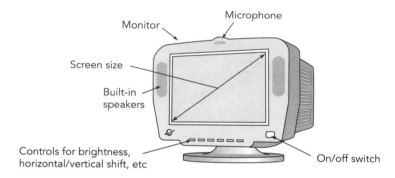

Monitor

Microphone

Screen size

Built-in speakers

Controls for brightness, horizontal/vertical shift, etc

On/off switch

A monitor

Computer monitors are similar in many ways to the television. They use cathode ray tubes (CRTs) containing an electron gun at the back of the tube which fires electrons at phosphor dots coating the inside of the screen. When struck by the electrons, the phosphor dots glow to give the colours. Because you sit very close to a computer screen and need to be able to read small text these dots need to be very close together. On a colour monitor a set of dots is made up of a group of three colours: one green, one blue and one red dot. One group of three dots is called a pixel (short for picture element) and a typical distance between the pixels on a computer monitor is 0.28 mm. The spacing of the pixels determines the clarity, or resolution, of the screen image, three standards in current use are:

- VGA (Video Graphics Array)   640 x 480 pixels

- SVGA (Super Video Graphics Array)   800 x 600 pixels

- XGA (Extended Graphics Array)   1024 x 768 pixels

Liquid crystal displays (LCDs)

 Liquid crystal displays are much smaller, lighter and use much less power than CRT-based monitors. Because of this they are used in notebook computers which are designed to be carried around by the user. However, to achieve the same quality of display incurs extra expense. LCDs are also used in watches and calculators.

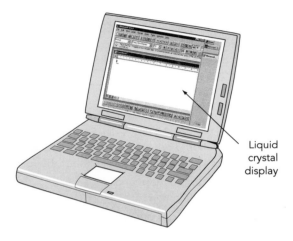

Liquid crystal display

Notebook computer

Light-emitting diodes (LEDs)

 LEDs are small electronic components which emit light when a voltage is placed across them. They are low power devices which can be seen on the front of a computer to show when the disk drive operates or when there is network activity.

LEDs are also used to monitor the logic state (ON and OFF) in control applications.

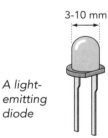

3-10 mm

A light-emitting diode

Over the years, many types of printers have been made with different print mechanisms. These printers can be placed in one of two groups -- impact printers and non-impact printers. With impact printers the letters, or tiny pins which make up characters, strike an inked ribbon against the paper. Because of this hammering effect these printers can be quite noisy. Today, the most popular types of printer for schools, offices and homes are ink-jet and laser printers, which are non-impact printers.

Dot-matrix printer

A dot-matrix printer has a print head that travels across the paper. In the head are a set of pins which shoot out and strike the ink ribbon against the paper as the print head moves along. These printers produce low to medium quality black and white printing and are relatively inexpensive (£150 upwards). Several years ago they were the ideal choice for a home printer but now the colour ink jet has taken their place. They are still used in business for the following reasons:

- They are cheap to purchase and running costs are very low.

- They are robust and can operate in harsh environments.

- If several sheets of self-carbonating paper are placed into the printer then multiple copies can be produced at the same time. This is because it is an impact printer and strikes the paper. This is particularly useful in places like warehouses.

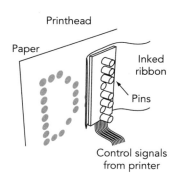

Ink-jet printer

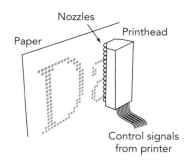

In an ink-jet printer the printhead contains tiny nozzles through which ink can be selectively sprayed onto the paper to form the characters or the graphic images. These printers are very quiet and can produce relatively high quality black and white or colour printing. Ink-jet printers cost from £100 upwards.

Laser printer

Laser printers work on the same principle as photocopiers. The toner, which is powdered ink, is transferred to the paper where it is fused by the action of heat and pressure. Lasers are silent printers and give high quality print. A school or business printer would have a typical speed of 8 to 16 pages per minute (ppm). Although laser printers can be purchased for less than £200, a faster, heavier duty machine would cost £1000 and upwards. The majority of laser printers sold are black and white, but colour laser printers are falling in price and becoming more popular.

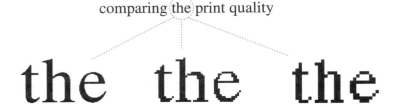

comparing the print quality

the the the

Plotters

There are several types of plotter. The flat-bed plotter, commonly found in the Design and Technology departments of schools, uses precision motors controlled by the computer. These motors move an arm across the paper in the 'x' direction and the pen unit up and down the arm in the 'y' direction. An electromagnet lifts and drops the pen onto the paper.

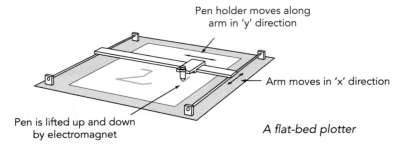

Pen holder moves along arm in 'y' direction

Arm moves in 'x' direction

Pen is lifted up and down by electromagnet

A flat-bed plotter

Plotters are often used in science and engineering applications for drawing building plans, printed circuit boards, machines and machine parts. They are accurate to hundredths of a millimetre and, although plotters found in schools may take A3 or A2 paper, flat-bed plotters can be the size of a small classroom.

Sound/voice

As well as having music played by the computer from programs or from CD-ROMs, it is also possible to have spoken output. This is particularly useful for blind users where passages of text or figures from a spreadsheet are spoken by the computer.

Switching

Earlier in this section we looked at how switches could be used as an input device. Computers can also output signals to switch equipment and machines on and off. This control of equipment requires much greater electrical power than can be provided by the computer. It is therefore necessary to boost the computers signal with special power switching electronic components.

Actuators

Signals from computers can generate physical movement in certain control devices. These devices are called actuators and include:

- motors
- hydraulics
- pneumatics
- solenoids.

Motors

The output of a computer can be used to drive small stepper motors. With stepper motors each electrical pulse from the computer rotates the motor shaft by a tiny amount. For a typical motor this might be a turn of 1.8° which would mean 200 pulses would be needed to turn the shaft of the motor through one complete revolution.

Stepper motors give very precise movements and can be used on devices such as flat-bed plotters or a robotic arm.

A stepper motor

Hydraulics

Here the output from the computer controls the movement of hydraulic rams by pumping oil. These hydraulic rams, similar to those seen on mechanical diggers and bulldozers, can be slow but are very powerful.

Pneumatics

Pneumatics are quite similar to hydraulics in using rams but the pistons are powered by air rather than oil. Pneumatics are not as powerful as the hydraulic systems but the movement of the system is very fast.

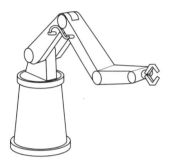

A robot arm can be controlled by motors, hydraulics or pneumatics. The type of system used depends on the application

Most accurate movement:	Motors
The fastest movement:	Pneumatics
Most powerful:	Hydraulics

Solenoids

Solenoids are coils of wire where, when electricity flows through them, the coil becomes an electromagnet and draws the shaft in the centre of the coil inward. Computers can output signals to operate the devices.

The movement of the solenoid can be used in many ways, eg to open latches and locks or to control the flow of gases and liquids in pipes.

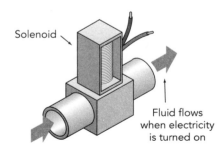

Solenoid

Fluid flows when electricity is turned on

Questions

1 Digital watches use microcomputers. Describe one input and one output device used.

   ....

   ....

2 Tick the device used for output from a computer:

   ☐ Joystick   ☐ Plotter

   ☐ Monitor   ☐ Bar code reader

3 Choose the best printer for the following situations:

   a A quiet, high quality, low cost, black and white printer for desktop publishing work.

   b A colour printer for use at home.

   c An impact printer that can print several copies at once using self-carbonating paper.

4 For each output device listed below give an example of where it might be used:

   a Speech from a voice chip

   ....

   b Stepper motor

   ....

   c LCD display

   ....

5 A laser printer is used with a desktop publishing program to print out text, diagrams and pictures for a leaflet. Give two reasons why a laser printer was chosen:

   a ....

   b ....

5 Computer memory

Bits

Computers are constructed of electronic circuits. Through these circuits there can be two states – electricity can be flowing or not flowing. When a pulse of electricity is present we call this a '1' and the absence of electricity is a '0'. The transistors on the silicon chips can store a 'bit' (**B**inary Dig**it**) which is either the '0' or the '1'.

Bytes

A byte is a unit of memory in the computer. It is made up of eight bits, in other words a byte can store eight '0s' or '1s'. Each character from the keyboard is given a code consisting of eight bits. These codes are the same internationally and are called the ASCII code (American Standard Code for Information Interchange). The code for the letter 'a' is 97 or 01100001. Each character therefore is held in one byte of memory. One byte is a very small amount of storage and it is more usual to refer to kilobytes (KB) and megabytes (MB).

- 1 kilobyte = 1024 bytes (2^{10})
- 1 megabyte = 1024 kilobytes = 1 048 576 bytes (2^{20})
  – approximately 1 million bytes.

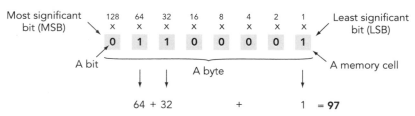

97 is the ASCII code for the lower-case letter 'a'.

How the letter 'a' is stored in computer memory

Methods used to store other types of data include:

- 2 to 4 bytes are required to store whole numbers (integers)
- 4 or 8 bytes are required to store real numbers (with decimals or fractions)
- 8 bytes are generally used to hold currency values and dates.

All computers have memory to store instructions and data. There are two main types of memory:

- RAM (Random access memory)
- ROM (Read only memory)

Random access memory (RAM)

The typical amount of RAM in a microcomputer might be 32 megabytes. When the computer is switched off this memory is empty. As the computer is started operating instructions, computer programs and data are moved into this memory as required.

The diagram on the right illustrates a memory map for the RAM. The RAM clears when the computer is switched off, which is why it is important to save your work to disk when you finish.

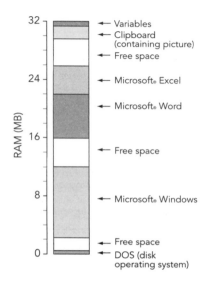

Read only memory (ROM)

ROM is memory stored in a chip which is not lost when the power is turned off.

On most computers (eg PCs) this memory is quite small but it contains the essential instructions to enable the computer to check the hardware and load operating systems from the disk in order to start.

Question

Complete the sentence below by using the correct words from the following list: *memory   megabytes   eight   RAM*

"A home computer has 32 .... of .... memory.

A byte is a unit of computer ....

It consists of .... bits."

6 Backing store

A 'backing store' retains its contents when the computer is switched off and is used to hold programs and data. Another name for backing store is secondary storage; all computers have some form of this storage.

Hard disks

Hard disks are a common form of backing store on most computers, both on stand-alone and networked computers. A typical microcomputer purchased for home or school would have a disk capacity of 1 Gigabyte (1024 Megabytes). This would hold the operating system (eg *Microsoft® Windows*), applications (word processor, spreadsheet, database, etc), games and the data from programs. On larger systems, the hard disks may hold Terabytes (1024 Gigabytes) of storage.

Data is stored by magnetising the surface of a flat circular plate. These plates rotate at high speed, typically 60 revolutions per second. A read/write head floats on a cushion of air a fraction of a millimetre above the surface of the disk. It is so close that even a smoke particle on the disk would cause the heads to crash. For this reason the drive is inside a sealed unit.

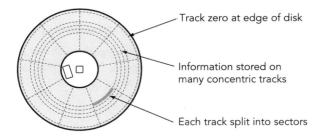

Tracks and sectors on a disk

Programs and data are held on the disk in blocks formed by tracks and sectors. Moving directly to data on a disk drive is called random access.

Floppy disks

Floppy disk drives can be found on most microcomputers and accept the familiar 3.5 inch floppy disks. High density disks for a PC hold 1.44 MB of data. Floppy disks are useful for transferring data between computers and for keeping a back-up of work files. Back-up disks should be kept safely away from the main computer for security reasons.

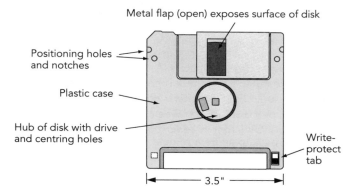

Metal flap (open) exposes surface of disk

Positioning holes and notches

Plastic case

Hub of disk with drive and centring holes

Write-protect tab

3.5"

Floppy disks only spin when loading or saving needs to take place. Floppy disks rotate more slowly than hard disks, at only six revolutions per second.

Disk access times

For a drive to read data from a disk, the read/write head must move in or out to align with the correct track. Then it must wait until the correct sector approaches the head. The time it takes to do this is called the disk access time or seek time. It sounds very short (about 10 milliseconds for a typical hard drive), but can be very significant when accessing or searching through large amounts of data (eg in a large database). Floppy disks and CD-ROMs have longer access times.

Compact discs

Computer compact discs hold huge quantities of data (650 Mb) in the form of text, sound, still pictures and video clips (see Chapter 10, page 66). The data is stored on the surface of the disc as minute indentations and is read by a laser light. The CDs are now available in three forms:

- **CD-ROMs** – The letters ROM in the name mean Read Only Memory – in other words you can only read from the disc, not write or store data onto it. This type is the most common sort of CD available and is the way most software programs are sold. It is a memory storage device but would not be considered as a 'backing store' as the user cannot write to the disc.

- **CD–R** – These CDs are initially blank but using a special Read/Write CD drive unit the user can store programs and data onto the disc. These discs can only be written to once.

- **CD–RW** – These are similar to the 'R' type above but the user can read, write and delete files from the disc many times, just like a hard disk.

Both the CD-ROMs and the CD-Rs can be referred to as a WORM device. This stands for **W**rite **O**nce **R**ead **M**any times.

Magnetic tape

Magnetic tape can also be used as a backing store for permanent storage. Data is saved along the tape in blocks, separated by 'interblock gaps'. Just like the tape in a tape-recorder, the data is written to or read from the tape as it passes the magnetic heads. One disadvantage of tape storage is that you cannot go directly to an item of data on the tape as you can with a disk. It is necessary to start at the beginning of the tape and search for the data as the tape goes past the heads – this is called serial access.

As magnetic tape is relatively cheap, tapes are often used to take a copy of hard disks for back-up (security) reasons. These tapes can then be kept in a safe place away from the computer.

Questions

1 Games programs can be purchased from computer stores on CD-ROM.

   a State two advantages of CD-ROMs over floppy disks.

   ....

   ....

   ....

   ....

   b State one disadvantage.

   ....

   ....

2 Hard disks and floppy disks are both used to store data from a computer. Give two instances where floppy disks are used.

   ....

   ....

All computers use an operating system (OS). This is a very complex program which controls the entire operation of the computer. It handles the BIOS (Basic Input Output Systems) like data from the keyboard and output to the screen and also the transfer of data to disk drives. Although the illustrations (see overpage) show different feature of operating systems, practical systems combine these features. For example, a sophisticated OS could handle multiprocessors, multiusers and multitasking simultaneously. Examples of three well-known operating systems are:

- UNIX – This operating system was written in the computing language C and is a multiuser, multitasking OS, often found on larger systems like minicomputers and mainframes.

- Microsoft. Windows 95 or 98 – a popular multitasking operating system used in PCs in homes, schools and in businesses.

- Windows. NT – a more complex multiuser/multitasking operating system used in network environments. If you are using Windows 95 on a school network then it is quite likely that the operating system being used by the network fileserver(s) is running a form of Windows NT.

Tasks of an operating system

We have already said that an operating system is a very complex program. Some of the tasks it needs to perform to ensure the efficient operation of the computer system include:

- allocating a slice of time with the CPU (central processing unit) for each job that needs to be processed

- ensuring that jobs with different priorities are dealt with in the correct order

- creating a balancing between tasks which require a lot of processing time with tasks needing more use of peripherals like printers

- always looking out for and handling interrupts like 'no paper in the printer'

- maximising use of the computer's memory by allocating different sections to the programs and data in use.

Methods of operation

There are a number of different ways in which computers are designed to operate. These include:

Single program mode – Just one program running on the computer at a time.

Multitasking (multiprogram) mode – Here two or more programs can be run at once. The operating system ensures that the resources of the computer are shared, including the processor where each program shares the processor time.

Multiuser mode – Here several users can use the same system together and the operating system gives each user a share of processor time called a time slice.

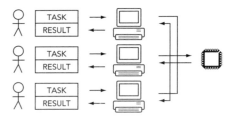

Multiprocessor mode – In larger systems the computer will contain more than one processor. The operating system allows the different processors to operate together and share the same memory.

Batch mode – It is sometime more efficient to collect together a group of programs or data, and then run this through the computer in one go or as a batch. An example of batch processing is running a payroll program. The wage data (eg hours worked) is batched together before the program is run to calculate the monthly wages. During batch processing there is no user input.

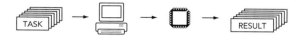

Realtime – Here the computer reacts immediately to incoming data and responds straightaway. These inputs might come from sensors in an aeroplane running on automatic pilot by computer. A change to the plane's flight caused by air currents must be corrected immediately. Another example of realtime processing would include making a reservation for the cinema or for a coach trip. When reserving the seat the computer will block others from taking the same seats even if they enquire a second later.

Computers running in realtime must be fast enough and have enough processing power to handle extreme situations.

Questions

1 Using the word list below, fill in the gaps in the following sentences:

> realtime   memory   multiuser/multitasking   printer
> multiprocessor   batch   mainframe

A computer that has more than one processor requires a

.... operating system. A network fileserver with one

processor requires a .... operating system.

When customers of a travel agent book their coach seats using the

Internet, this form of processing is called ....

When the travel agents calculate the monthly wages for their staff they

are more likely to use .... processing.

2 Which of the following situations does not use realtime processing?

   a   an embedded computer-controlled washing machine

   b   asking directory enquiries for a telephone number

   c   a flight simulator package

   d   printing a telephone directory.

8 Human–computer interface

The way in which a computer user communicates with the computer is called the human–computer interface (or man–machine interface).

A good interface between the user and the computer program should be:

- friendly – being able to use the software/program without needing to read the whole manual first

- attractive – encourages users to use the software

- effective – it does the job it is designed to do efficiently

- easy to use – menu structures are consistent across packages (eg to save a program users expect to find the option under the 'File' drop-down menu).

Graphical user interface (GUI)

One form in common use is the Graphical User Interface or GUI system (pronounced Gooey). Small pictures or icons representing actions are displayed and can be selected with the mouse. The use of 'windows' makes the operation of programs easier.

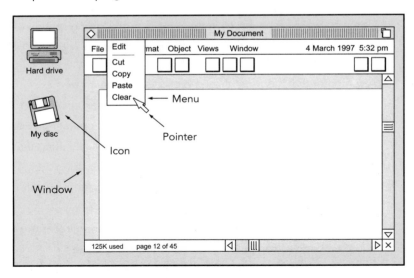

The screen may display several windows for different applications but only the one currently in use will be active. Another term used for this form of interface is WIMP (Windows, Icons, Menus and Pointer).

Command line interface

It is possible to give the computer instructions without the aid of menus and icons. This is done by typing the instructions directly into the computer so that they can be seen on screen. This has the disadvantage that the user must know the commands to type in. The advantage is that quite specific instructions can be given directly.

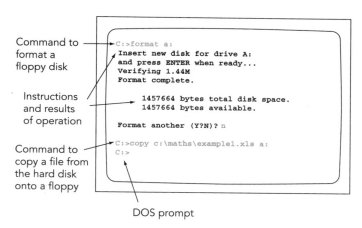

Command to format a floppy disk

Instructions and results of operation

Command to copy a file from the hard disk onto a floppy

```
C:>format a:
Insert new disk for drive A:
and press ENTER when ready...
Verifying 1.44M
Format complete.

     1457664 bytes total disk space.
     1457664 bytes available.

Format another (Y?N)? n

C:>copy c:\maths\example1.xls a:
C:>
```

DOS prompt

Questions

1 A package is described as 'mouse driven'.

   a Explain what this term means.

   ....

   b State two features you would expect to find when using the package.

   ....

   ....

2 In graphical user interfaces the choices available in the drop-down menus are 'greyed' or 'ghosted' out and cannot be selected. Explain why this might occur and give an example.

   ....

   ....

9 Software packages

Software is the general name for programs that are suitable for a range of purposes, from writing a letter to controlling a set of traffic lights. There are four particular software application packages that are widely used in homes, schools and in business. These are:

- word processors (used to produce letters, reports, projects, books)

- desktop publishing (used to design leaflets, advertisements, posters)

- databases (used to store, sort, search and retrieve information)

- spreadsheets (used for calculations, forecasting and modelling)

The illustration below shows how a uniform shop in a school might use each of these four software packages:

The uniform shop needs to purchase the different clothes (blazers, shirts, trousers, ties, sports wear, etc) from the manufacturers. A database is kept of all the goods held in the uniform shop including the type of garment, the size and the number in stock. This helps to:

- monitor stock levels and print out reports

- reorder new stock before items run out of stock

- search the database for items of uniform when parents enquire.

The school may wish to make a small profit from the shop and so a spreadsheet is used to calculate the selling price for each item, also the monthly and yearly sales figures. A word processor is used to write letters to parents, place orders with the suppliers and prepare the price lists each term. The desktop publishing package is used to produce posters advertising the uniform shop, and the days and times it opens.

The clipboard

One important feature of using application packages in a Windows® environment is the ability to cut (or copy) and paste between packages. The sections of work that have been selected (highlighted) can be cut or copied and then pasted into another position in the document, into another document or into another application package. When the cut or copy option is used, the selected material is held in a part of the memory referred to as the 'clipboard'. Only one selection can be held in the clipboard at a time, so if another cut or copy is done the first selection is lost from the clipboard.

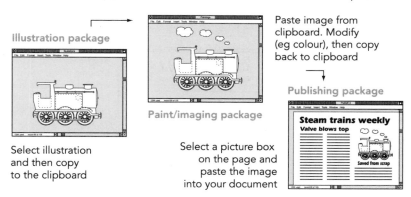

Illustration package

Paste image from clipboard. Modify (eg colour), then copy back to clipboard

Publishing package

Paint/imaging package

Select illustration and then copy to the clipboard

Select a picture box on the page and paste the image into your document

Macros

A macro is a way of recording and storing a sequence of keystrokes or instructions. These can then be 'played back' when required by running the stored macro. A macro facility can often be found in word processors, databases and spreadsheets and can help to reduce the time taken for repetitive tasks or help the user to perform more complex instructions. For example, a macro might be set up in a:

- Word processor – to insert your name and address at the top of a page.

- Database – to carry out instructions to search for certain records, sort them into order and then print the records out.

- Spreadsheet – to carry out instructions to draw a graph of some results.

Once a macro has been recorded it is given a name and stored. It can then be activated by either a combination of key presses (known as hot keys), eg CTRL + J or by placing a button on the screen.

Word processing

A word processor can be used to write letters, reports, essays, projects, memos, curriculum vitae, theses – any form of written work. When text is entered at the keyboard the characters and words are displayed on the screen and held in the computer's memory. This work can be saved to disk and printed.

The advantage of using a word processor is that the text can be changed (edited) on the screen and reprinted if mistakes are made. The word processor also has many features which can be used to format the document.

Formatting

When we format a document we choose the way it looks. We might put characters into **bold**, *italic*, <u>underlined</u> or CAPITAL letters. We might alter the spacing between letters and lines or set the writing out in columns or tables.

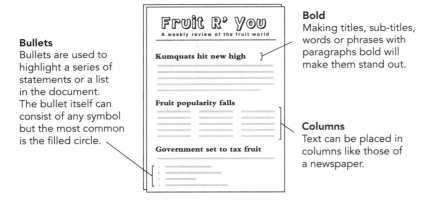

Bullets
Bullets are used to highlight a series of statements or a list in the document. The bullet itself can consist of any symbol but the most common is the filled circle.

Bold
Making titles, sub-titles, words or phrases with paragraphs bold will make them stand out.

Columns
Text can be placed in columns like those of a newspaper.

Fonts

This is the name we give to styles of print. There are many different fonts. Two quite common fonts are Times Roman and Helvetica:

Thickness (line weights) vary considerably

Clearly visible serifs

No serifs

Thickness more consistent

Fonts can be broadly grouped into serif and sans serif fonts. Serifs on a character are the cross-strokes that cap the strokes which make up a character. In the illustration on the previous page you will see that the Times Roman font has serifs but the Helvetica font does not. Serifs help the eye flow along the line as the words are read and serif fonts are often used in newspapers and magazines. Sans serif fonts can be used on application forms, for example, where the eye of the reader needs to be drawn to each box in turn.

Justification

There are four ways in which text can lie in a column and at any stage the user can alter all or part of the document to any one of the four. These are illustrated below.

For justification, where the text is lined up to both the left- and right-hand edges, the program checks, line by line, the length of the text. If it is less than the line length, it stretches the text by spreading the letters and words, or by inserting additional spaces.

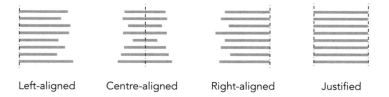

| Left-aligned | Centre-aligned | Right-aligned | Justified |

Tabs

Tabs are often used for setting out tables or columns. Tab positions can be set across the page. Then, when the tab key on the keyboard is pressed, the cursor (flashing bar) will jump to the next tab position across the page.

The four most common types of tab markers: left tabs, right tabs, centre tabs and decimal tabs are shown below:

Centre tab	Left tab	Right tab	Decimal tab
↓	↲	↲	↓
Resistor	0.22 ohms	6z – 0100	£0.12
Capacitor	56 pF	08 – 0495	£0.07
Relay	5V DC 80R	60 – 585	£1.10
Semiconductor	3A+5V	LM 323 K	£2.40
Tools	Precision Drill	85 – 55	£29.70

Style sheets

A style sheet holds information about the parts of a document: the body of the text, chapter titles, headings and subheadings, footers and headers, etc. Each style sheet might contain information on the font to be used, the size, alignment, spacings, colour, background, border, shading, etc. Once style sheets have been set up for a document they are very easy to apply. Highlight the particular text, eg a heading, then select the heading style from the menu list. The advantages of using style sheets in documents are:

- it is quick to apply a range of formatting to the highlighted text

- with long documents it makes it easy to be consistent, ie all the titles, subtitles, etc having the same style throughout the document

- marking text with the heading style will allow the word processor to automatically create a 'contents' page in longer documents

- it makes it very easy to change formats throughout the whole document.

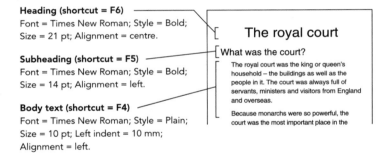

A typical style sheet setup

Setting up a page

Landscape or portrait

Ordinary A4 paper (29.7 cm x 21 cm) can be printed in two orientations, known as portrait and landscape. As shown below, portrait is printed with the longest side vertical, this is the usual (default) setting. Alternatively, landscape can be selected which prints with the longest side horizontally. Landscape orientation can be useful when designing an A5 booklet where the A4 page will be folded, or for wide tables, illustrations and use of columns.

Portrait   Landscape

Headers

Headers allow the user to specify text which will automatically be printed at the top of each page. The position across the page, and the style and size of the header text can be specified. Items that might be placed in a header include the description of the document or the chapter number.

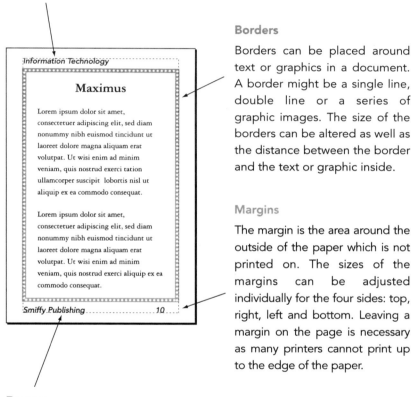

Borders

Borders can be placed around text or graphics in a document. A border might be a single line, double line or a series of graphic images. The size of the borders can be altered as well as the distance between the border and the text or graphic inside.

Margins

The margin is the area around the outside of the paper which is not printed on. The sizes of the margins can be adjusted individually for the four sides: top, right, left and bottom. Leaving a margin on the page is necessary as many printers cannot print up to the edge of the paper.

Footers

A footer, as the name implies, is found at the foot of the page. As with headers, once the layout of a footer is defined for all or part of a document it will appear on each printed page. The footer often contains the page number which is automatically increased through the document.

Editing

Spell-check

A useful facility for many people! The 'spell-check' makes use of an extensive dictionary held on the disk. Each word in your document is compared with words in the dictionary and the user is invited to 'change' or 'ignore' words selected by the spell-checker. When words in the document are not found in the dictionary the spell-checker will suggest words that have similar spellings or that sound similar when spoken.

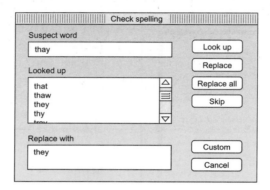

Spell-check box

Often spell-checkers have the facility to create dictionaries for the user for special words. These words might include real names, address names, postcodes and technical words not normally found in a dictionary. Dictionaries are also available for specialist subjects like medicine.

Grammar check

This check will look at the way each sentence in the document is written and compares it with a set of rules for grammar and style of writing. The user can usually select how strictly these rules are applied to their work. The grammar check will suggest ways in which the sentence can be improved if it varies from the rules. The check often includes statistics on readability: based on the number of syllables in words, the length of words and the number of words in sentences, the reading age can be determined. 'Standard' writing averages 17 words per sentence and 147 syllables per 100 words.

Modern wordprocessors check the spelling and grammar as the words are entered, indicating errors with coloured lines.

Thesaurus

This is very useful when you can't think of quite the right word to use in a document. Select a word, or phrase, and the thesaurus will display a range of words with the same or similar meanings. For example, using the phrase 'similar to' in the thesaurus produces:

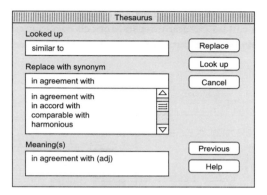

An example of a thesaurus enquiry

Mailmerge

The diagram below illustrates the process of a mailmerge operation. This is often used to produce personalised letters and is achieved having a single standard letter with links to a data source. When the mailmerge process is started, items of data are inserted into the standard letter before being printed. The process is then repeated for the next set of data until all the letters have been generated.

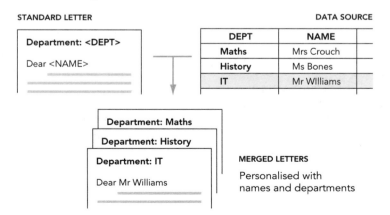

Desktop publishing (DTP)

A desktop publishing program allows users to look at the page of the document as a whole and design the layout by marking areas for text and graphics. Text can be arranged in columns with large titles or headlines heading the columns. Images can be imported from graphics packages, scanned, digitised or taken from clipart libraries on the disk or CD-ROM. All these features can be put together to produce newspapers, newsletters, pages for books, posters, brochures, leaflets, prospectuses, etc.

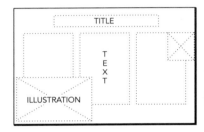 

Design   Finished page

Graphics

Documents often require graphics such as pictures and images to illustrate the text. These can be obtained from:

- clipart libraries supplied with the word processing and DTP packages
- clipart libraries supplied separately on disks
- drawing and painting packages, where images are created by the user
- using a scanner
- using a digitiser
- CD-ROMs
- digital cameras.

Once the image is displayed on the computer screen, the user can manipulate the image by resizing, rotating, shearing and cropping. These terms are explained on the next page.

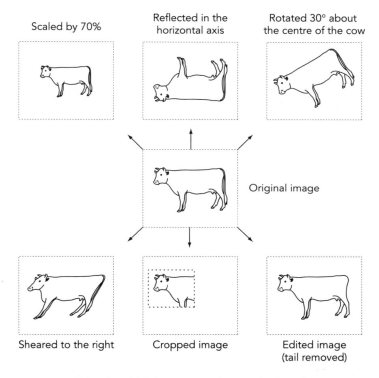

Scaled by 70%

Reflected in the horizontal axis

Rotated 30° about the centre of the cow

Original image

Sheared to the right

Cropped image

Edited image (tail removed)

Ways in which images can be manipulated

Layering

When pictures are positioned over text or text is placed over pictures in a document this is called layering. In order to create the effect required it may be necessary to select the object and 'Send to Back' or 'Bring to Front'. It is also possible to make the text background transparent so that the picture or image can be seen behind the text.

Milk

Milk is a good source of the essential vitamins and minerals required to keep the body healthy

Milk

Milk is a good source of the essential vitamins and minerals required to keep the body healthy

Objects in layers can be moved 'on top' of each other

Databases

A database is a collection of related data items, which are linked and structured so that the data can be accessed in a number of ways.

A simple database consists of only one set of data. This is called a flat file. An example of a flat file database is *Pinpoint* or *Microsoft® Works*.

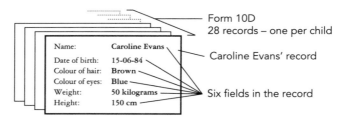

A relational database is more complex (see page 45). Relational databases are very powerful as they allow the data to be accessed in many different ways. An example of a relational database is *Microsoft® Access*.

In larger databases there will be many users accessing the data at the same time. These databases need complex software called Database Management Systems (DBMS) to allow this.

Functions of a database

A database program on a computer is designed to hold information (data). Often the amount of information stored is very large and it would take a long time for us to search through this information if it were written on paper. Holding the information in a database enables us to search very quickly and to sort the information easily. The required data can then be printed out as a report.

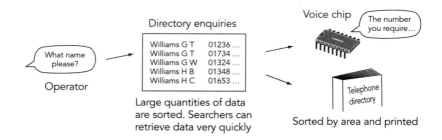

An example database

Suppose we wished to create a books database. Each student in the class is asked to bring in details of ten books from home. These details will then be added to the class database. Using this database we could examine the selection of books to determine the:

- most popular publisher
- most popular author
- average number of pages
- average number of chapters
- average number of pages per chapter
- average cost of the books
- most/least popular books.

Typical information for a book might include:

> *The Worst Witch All At Sea* is written by Jill Murphy and published by Penguin Books. Its ISBN is 0 670 83253 7. It costs £8.99, has 21 chapters and 222 pages. I thought it was excellent and gave it a rating of 9 out of 10.

In our computer database each book would make up a record. Within the record the details of the book is structured into fields (see page 46).

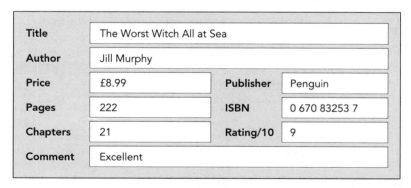

Structuring the data in this way enables the database program to search, sort, display and print the data easily. With the data now contained in specific fields, if we wished to search for the book with the most pages we would instigate a search of the 'Number of pages' field in each record throughout the database. Structuring the data also enables us to see if a field is empty and whether or not important information is missing.

Sorting

Being able to sort the data is a very important function of a database package. The steps involved in sorting data are listed below:

Example

1   Select the field you wish to use to sort by; this might be a 'Surname' field or 'Account number' field. Sometimes you may wish to choose a secondary field to sort by. For example, if the main sort is by surname, a secondary sort would be by first name in case there were several people with the same surname.

2   Decide whether the list should be in ascending ('A' at the top and 'Z' at the bottom) or descending order.

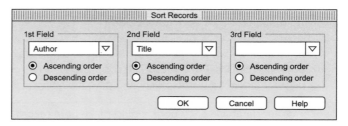

Here the instructions given to the database are to do a main sort by author and a secondary sort by the title of the book

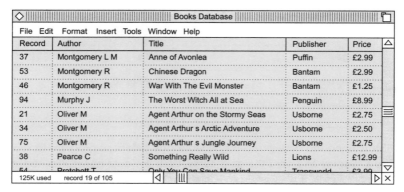

The sorted data is now by author and then title

Note: When you do a sort, numbers come before capital letters which come before lower-case letters.

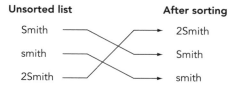

Unsorted list	After sorting
Smith	2Smith
smith	Smith
2Smith	smith

Searching

To be able to retrieve information from a database, particularly from a large database, is vitally important. This is done by the computer taking the user's request and searching for a match in the database. The steps necessary to carry out a search are:

1 Choose the 'query' or 'find' option.

2 Specify which field in the record you wish to search.

3 Decide the condition statement:
> 'is equal to'
> 'is greater than'
> 'is not equal to'
> 'is less than or equal to'
> 'is greater than or equal to'
> 'contains'.

4 Enter the value to be searched for.

5 If another condition needs to be applied to the search, go back to step 2; otherwise start the search.

Example

1 If we were searching the books database to find a book with 'witches' and 'wizards' in the title, we might use the following search:

Title 'contains' "Witch"

OR

Title 'contains' "Wizard"

Note: The use of the condition 'contains' will find the word as part of the title and will also find "Witches" and "Wizards"

2   To search for a highly rated (rating of 10) and cheap book (£5 or less) we might use the search:

Rating 'is equal to' 10
AND
Price 'is less than or equal to' 5

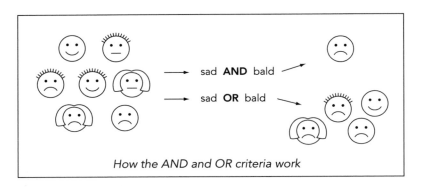

sad **AND** bald

sad **OR** bald

How the AND and OR criteria work

Database forms

When you are entering data into a database you can design the layout by placing boxes and labels on to the screen where the data is to be typed into the different fields. These data input screens are often referred to as forms.

Database reports

Database reports can be designed by the user to show the data or, more usually, print out data from the database. When creating a report the user can choose whether all or just some of the fields in the database record are to be printed. Data can be printed in columns and numeric fields can be totalled at the bottom of each page and at the end of the report.

Relational databases

The type of database shown earlier in this section is called a flat file database. The data is held in a single file and the sorting, searching and printing of reports is done on this data file. This sort of database is suitable for use at home or in a school but it would not be adequate for larger businesses and organisations. Here a large amount of data is required and it is necessary to separate the data into tables with each table holding data relating to one subject or entity.

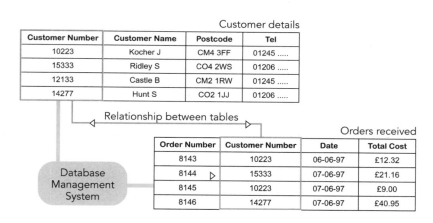

Customer details

Customer Number	Customer Name	Postcode	Tel
10223	Kocher J	CM4 3FF	01245 .....
15333	Ridley S	CO4 2WS	01206 .....
12133	Castle B	CM2 1RW	01245 .....
14277	Hunt S	CO2 1JJ	01206 .....

Relationship between tables

Orders received

Order Number	Customer Number	Date	Total Cost
8143	10223	06-06-97	£12.32
8144	15333	07-06-97	£21.16
8145	10223	07-06-97	£9.00
8146	14277	07-06-97	£40.95

Database Management System

In relational databases data is grouped into tables

In relational databases the tables of data exist independently from the programs which may use them. The Database Management System (DBMS) provides the software tools to link the tables together and do searches of the data. Each user may have a different view of the database, with restricted data only being accessible to those with the necessary authority. Different departments and individuals can be given permission to edit and update parts of the data. For example, the sales department may be given the task of ensuring the customer data is kept up-to-date.

An example of a relational database on a local area network using microcomputers is *Microsoft₀ Access*, which is available in many schools. On larger commercial systems examples of relational databases include *Oracle* and *SQLServer*.

Database fields

Each 'record' of a database contains 'fields' where the data or information is stored. When a new database is being designed, many database packages request the user to specify the type of data that will be entered into each of the fields. This allows the computer to process the data effectively and allocate computer memory efficiently.

Different types of field include:

- Alphanumeric/text field – letters or numbers, eg 'Car registration' = N741GEV

- Numeric field – numbers which can be used for statistics or calculations. Numeric fields can be divided further into 'integer' fields (numbers without decimal places) and 'real' numbers (with decimal places). For example, 'Age' = 15 or 'Price' = 12.95.

- Data/time field – these fields are specifically designed to store dates and times which can then be displayed in different formats, eg 2 April 1952 might be displayed in the form:

d-mmmm-yyyy	= 2 April 1952
dd-mmm-yy	= 02-Apr-52
dd-mm-yy	= 02-04-52

  Holding dates in a date field allows searches to take place, eg show records where 'Last payment date' greater than 1 November.

- Calculation field – this is used when the field displays a calculation based on numbers in other fields.

  For example, 'Area of circle' = 3.142 x ('Radius field')^2.

- Picture/image field – Many modern databases now have a field where pictures can be displayed within the record. The data entered into this field by the user would include file details of the image to be displayed.

Information and data

The two words 'information' and 'data' often seem to mean the same thing. We put information into computers which is stored as data. There is, however, a subtle difference between the two. If, for example, the data in a computer was '02041952', what would this mean? Is it a part number? An account number? A telephone number? If you know it is a date, then we understand it means 2 April 1952.

Information = Data + 'The context and structure of the data'

Coding information

It is sometimes useful to code information in database fields. Say, for example, we were entering our subjects studied at school, we might code these as:

MA = Maths   EN = English
FR = French   DT = Design and Technology

Advantages:

- easier and quicker to enter
- less typing required
- less likely to make spelling mistakes
- uses less computer memory
- allows fixed length fields (see below).

Fixed length records

When a database has fixed length records, then each field within the record is allocated a fixed number of bytes.

Advantages:

- It is easier for the computer to process because if you edit a field and save the record back to the disk it will take up exactly the same space as before.
- It makes locating a particular record very rapid as the position for the start of each record is known.

Disadvantage:

- If data is too long to fit into a field it must be abbreviated and if it is shorter that the space allocated then memory is being wasted.

Fixed length records

| T | h | e | | W | o | r | s | t | | W | i | t | c | h | | A | l | l | | a | t | | S | e | a | | |
| J | i | l | l | | M | u | r | p | h | y | | | | | | | | | | | | | | | | | | |

Variable length records

| T | h | e | | W | o | r | s | t | | W | i | t | c | h | | A | l | l | | a | t | | S | e | a | # | J |
| i | l | l | | M | u | r | p | h | y | # | £ | 8 | . | 9 | 9 | # | P | e | n | g | u | i | n | | B | o | o |

     # = end of field marker

How data is stored for fixed and variable length records

Variable length records

Here the fields in a record can vary in size and even the number of fields can vary. As the field and record size is not set, special characters (end of field markers and end of record markers) must be inserted to show the ends.

Advantages:

- Useful where databases hold mainly text.
- Memory is not wasted by empty spaces.

Disadvantages:

- More difficult for the computer to process.
- Lengthening a field entry while editing may mean the record cannot be saved back onto the disk in the original position.

Key fields

The key field is the one used to identify each record and is often used when searching and sorting the records. If the record contains a field like an account number and this is a unique number only for that record, then this field is called the primary key field. If there is not a unique primary key then the key field can be formed from several fields, eg 'First address line' and 'Postcode'. This is called a composite key.

Data capture

If we are going to search and sort data in a database then it is necessary to capture the data first. This can be done using any of the input devices mentioned in Chapter 3, although some are more commonly used than others.

Using a questionnaire to gather data and entering this via the keyboard is still one of the most common methods.

Questionnaire

Please complete all sections, using block capitals where appropriate.

Name

Form

Subject	A	B	C	D	E
Mathematics	☐	☐	☐	☐	☐
English	☐	☐	☐	☐	☐
Science	☐	☐	☐	☐	☐
History	☐	☐	☐	☐	☐
Geography	☐	☐	☐	☐	☐
Technology	☐	☐	☐	☐	☐
French	☐	☐	☐	☐	☐
Physical Education	☐	☐	☐	☐	☐

Please indicate your view of the subject
A = very interesting; E= very dull

Page 1

Validation

This is the name given to the checks a computer can carry out when data is input. Whatever form of input device is used some form of check can be made on the data entering the computer.

Example: A database field in a secondary school timetable package contains information about the teacher, subject and year group. This information is coded as follows:

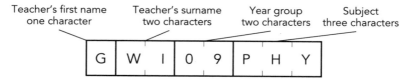

Teacher's first name one character | Teacher's surname two characters | Year group two characters | Subject three characters

G W I 0 9 P H Y

This shows the code entered for Mr G Williams teaching Physics to Year 9. Here are some checks to make sure that the data has been entered correctly:

Presence check: The field cannot be left empty when completing the record.

You have not entered a class code. This field must contain data.

OK

Character count: There should always be eight characters in this field; more or less would prompt the user to edit the data.

G W I 0 9 P

Range check: The fourth and fifth characters are extracted from the code and converted to a number. The validation check then ensures that the number is 'equal to or greater than' 7 AND 'less than or equal to' 13 (assuming the school has a sixth form).

$$7 \leq 09 \leq 13 ?$$

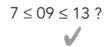

File lookup: Here the teacher's code (first three characters) and the subject code (last three characters) can be checked by opening separate files and ensuring the codes do exist in a valid list.

G WILLIAMS

GWI

Picture check: This checks that the data entered in this field is as expected, ie TTTNNTTT (where T = text and N = number).

GWI09PHY
=
TTTNNTTT

There are also a number of totalling checks that can be carried out when processing data. Take, for example, a payroll program which is run at the end of each month to calculate the wages. The hours worked by each employee is input to disk in preparation for running the payroll program. At the front of the data, in a batch header record, several extra pieces of information can be included. These enable the computer program to check the data being entered and report any errors. This data includes:

- Batch totals: How many records are being processed
- Control totals: A manually calculated figure, eg the total hours worked
- Hash totals: A total, often quite meaningless, figure calculated by the computer, eg the sum of all the employee numbers.

These checks help ensure that the program processes the payroll accurately and that no employees are left out or are paid incorrectly.

Check digits

Some numbers are given an extra digit on the end which is called a check digit. This digit is calculated from the original number and acts as a check when the number is read by the computer. There are several ways in which these check digits are calculated. One popular method is called the modulus-11 method. An example of how the check digit is calculated is shown below:

1 Multiply each digit in the number by a factor, starting with two and going up by one.

Original number	1	2	3	4
	x	x	x	x
Multiply factors	5	4	3	2

$5 + 8 + 9 + 8 = 30$

2 Add the products together

3 Divide the total by 11 $30 \div 11 = 2$ remainder 8

4 Subtract the remainder from 11 to obtain the check digit*. $11 - 8 = 3$ (check digit)

The new number, including its check digit becomes **1234 3**

*There are two special cases; if the remainder is '1' the check digit is 'X'. If the remainder is '0' the check digit is '0'.

When the computer reads the number (including the check digit) it checks the calculation and gives an error message if it is not correct. This procedure may seem complicated but it traps 99% of common errors like getting two digits mixed up.

Numbers that use check digits include customer account numbers, International Standard Book Numbers (ISBNs) and the numbers on bar codes. You may have noticed at the checkout till of the supermarket that some products have to be passed several times across the scanner before the beep tells the assistant it has been read correctly. Each time a product is scanned the number associated with the black and white lines is validated using the check digit.

Questions

1   Mr Yap is a dentist and keeps records of his patients in a database so that he can send out reminder letters every six months. Which of the following fields would be included?

a   ☐   Date of last appointment

b   ☐   Patient's address

c   ☐   How much the patient earns

d   ☐   Type of car the patient drives

2   A bank holds a database for its customers. List four fields that it might hold in the database about its customers:

a   ....   b   ....

c   ....   d   ....

3   Complete the following sentences by inserting the correct word from the list given below:

file   fields   key   customer   unique

"There is one record for each .... on the bank's customer

database .... Each record consists of ....

giving details of the customer. Each customer is given a

.... account number with the bank; this is called the

.... field."

4   The third set of Physics pupils is taught by Mr G Williams and is coded in a database as:

  • First three letters of the subject
  • A number for the set
  • First letter of the teacher's first name
  • First two letters of the teacher's surname

The code is: PHY3GWI

What is the code for the following groups:

a   The second Geography set with Mrs F Long? ....

b   The first Art class with Miss E McVeigh? ....

c   Give one reason why codes are used in databases.

   ....

5   A school library uses databases to hold information on books and users. Some of these databases are on CD-ROM and some are kept on the hard drive of the computer.

a   What data is likely to be held on the CD-ROM?

   ....

   ....

b   Give one advantage of using a CD-ROM.

   ....

   ....

c   Give one advantage of using a hard drive.

   ....

   ....

6   A company adds a record to a data file whenever it sells to a new customer. State one validation check used when the number of the month of first sale is entered

   ....

   ....

Spreadsheets

A spreadsheet is a computer program which is designed to display and process numbers. It is made up of a grid into which numbers are entered. The program contains many mathematical, statistical and financial calculations which can be applied to the numbers. Many spreadsheets can also show the numbers in the form of graphs.

A spreadsheet is a very useful and powerful tool for experimenting with numbers and asking 'What if ...?' (see page 57).

The illustration below shows a screen from a typical spreadsheet program. Each column of cells has a letter at the top and each row has a number on the left. By using the letter for the column and the number for the row we can address each cell individually. We can move from one cell to another by entering the new cell address, using the arrow keys on the keyboard or by pointing and clicking with the mouse.

Editing bar

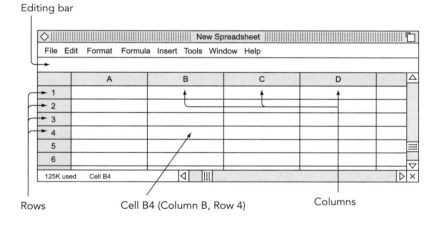

Rows
Cell B4 (Column B, Row 4)
Columns

Contents of the cell

Cells in the spreadsheet may contain numbers, text (letters, words, etc), dates and formulas. Each cell, or a block of cells, may be 'formatted' so that the contents of the cell is displayed in different ways.

The way a number appears in the cell is controlled through formatting the cell. For example, to display £12.50, then:

• Enter 12.5

• Highlight the cell (or the row or column)

• Now format the cell to display currency with two decimal places.

Number
24.3 is entered and then formatted £###0.00.
The cell then displays £24.30

Date
5.2.97 is entered and then formatted as dd-mmm-yyyy.
Displayed as 05-Feb-1997

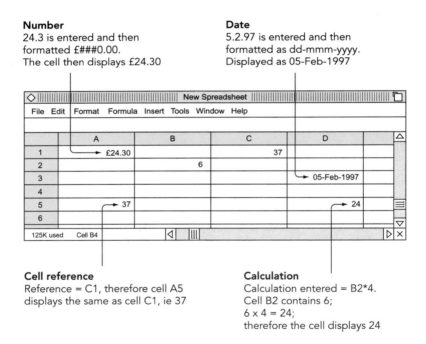

Cell reference
Reference = C1, therefore cell A5 displays the same as cell C1, ie 37

Calculation
Calculation entered = B2*4.
Cell B2 contains 6;
6 x 4 = 24;
therefore the cell displays 24

When a cell is selected, the contents of the cell are shown on the editing bar but the result of any calculation is displayed in the cell.

The illustration below shows some of the different ways numbers can be formatted in the cells of a spreadsheet.

Format	Example*	Description
0	12346	integer
0.00	12345.68	2 decimal places
#,##0	12,346	integer with thousands separator
£0.00	£12345.68	pounds and pence
0%	1234568%	integer percentage
0.00E+00	1.23E+04	3 significant figures plus exponent

*Example shows how the number 12345.6789 would be displayed in the various formats

Calculations

The power of a spreadsheet comes from its ability to do calculations with numbers. The contents of one cell can be calculated from other cells in the sheet.

Formula = A2*B2.

Sometimes when students see this kind of spreadsheet they want to type the answer '12' straight into cell C2. Cell C2 should contain A2*B2. If the number in cell A2 or B2 is now changed the new area will automatically be calculated in cell C2.

Formulae (functions)

Spreadsheet packages come with a library of formulae and functions as part of the program. There are formulae for financial calculations, for handling dates and times, for mathematical and statistical work and for logical expressions. In the example given overpage just two of the many functions are illustrated, the SUM function and the IF statement.

An example of using a function to show the results of an examination is given below. The pass mark is 40% and the formulae in the right-hand column shows whether the student has passed or failed.

	A	B	C	D	E	D	E
1			Paper 1	Paper 2	Paper 3	Total	PASS/
2			(30%)	(30%)	(40%)	(%)	FAIL
3	Katie-Marie	NORMAN	12	14	20	=SUM(C3:E3)	=IF(F3>39,"PASS", "FAIL")
4	Noel	LUFF	4	5	15	=SUM(C4:E4)	=IF(F4>39,"PASS", "FAIL")
5	Catherine	OAKLEY	15	19	27	=SUM(C5:E5)	=IF(F5>39,"PASS", "FAIL")
6	Laura	ODD	9	13	30	=SUM(C6:E6)	=IF(F6>39,"PASS", "FAIL")
7	Matthew	LAWRIE	13	9	17	=SUM(C7:E7)	=IF(F7>39,"PASS", "FAIL")

The IF function

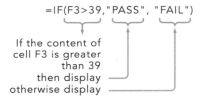

=IF(F3>39,"PASS", "FAIL")

If the content of
cell F3 is greater
than 39
then display
otherwise display

The SUM function

=SUM(C3:E3)

Add up the content
of cells C3 to E3
(ie C3+D3+E3)

	A	B	C	D	E	D	E
1			Paper 1	Paper 2	Paper 3	Total	PASS/
2			(30%)	(30%)	(40%)	(%)	FAIL
3	Katie-Marie	NORMAN	12	14	20	46	PASS
4	Noel	LUFF	4	5	15	24	FAIL
5	Catherine	OAKLEY	15	19	27	61	PASS
6	Laura	ODD	9	13	30	52	PASS
7	Matthew	LAWRIE	13	9	17	39	FAIL

Recalculation

Often the contents of some cells in a spreadsheet are dependent on others. For instance, in the example on page 55 cell C2 depends on the values in A2 and B2. When the contents of a cell is changed the spreadsheet will need to recalculate the values in all the other cells. This recalculation can be set to automatic or manual:

- automatic – the sheet recalculates after every cell entry
- manual – recalculation only takes place when selected by the user.

For a small spreadsheet automatic recalculation is easiest. For larger, more complex sheets the recalculation can take several seconds so it is more convenient to switch to manual mode for faster data entry. (Note: It can also make a difference as to how the sheet recalculates, whether by working along the rows or down the columns first.)

'What if...?'

This is a phrase often associated with spreadsheets. If a number in one cell is changed then the value in another cell may also change since it uses the first number in a calculation. The second cell may change a third cell and so on through the sheet. The values in your spreadsheet model can be recalculated instantly when you change the contents of individual cells, for example 'What if the price is increased to ...?', 'What if the sales fall by ...?', 'What if the VAT rate changes to ...?', etc.

Constructing a spreadsheet

The sheet below shows the sales from the school tuck shop for a week:

	A	B	C	D	E	F
1		Crisps	Mars bars	Snickers	Apples	
2	Mon	17	22	12	11	
3	Tue	23	19	7	14	
4	Wed	24	16	8	9	
5	Thu	18	17	9	11	
6	Fri	21	16	13	12	
7	Total sold					
8						
9	Sale price	25	30	25	20	
10	Cost price	20	24	18	10	
11						
12	Total sales					
13	Total costs					
14						
15	Weekly profit					

1   In column F we can total the number of items sold each day. In cell F2 we would use the formula =sum(b2:e2). After entering this the cell F2 would display the answer 62. To insert this calculation for Tuesday to Friday in cells F3 to F6 we copy or replicate the calculation in F2.

2   In row 7 we can total the individual items sold during the week. In cell B7 we would enter the formula =sum(b2:b6). We would then copy this formula into cells C7 to E7.

3   To find how much money or income we have made from the sales of each item we need to add a formula to the cells in row 12. In B12 the formula is =B7xB9; this will work out how much money we have made during the week from the sale of crisps.

4   The items sold at the tuck shop need to be purchased by the school. Row 10 of the sheet shows the cost for each item. In row 13 we need to show the total costs for the items sold during the week. The formula for this is =B7xB10.

	A	B	C	D	E	F
1		Crisps	Mars bars	Snickers	Apples	
2	Mon	17	22	12	11	62
3	Tue	23	19	7	14	63
4	Wed	24	16	8	9	57
5	Thu	18	17	9	11	55
6	Fri	21	16	13	12	62
7	Total sold	103	90	49	57	
8						
9	Sale price	25	30	25	20	
10	Cost price	20	24	18	10	
11						
12	Total sales	2575	2700	1225	1140	
13	Total costs	2060	2160	882	570	
14						
15	Weekly profit	515	540	343	570	

5   The profit is the difference between the selling price and the buying price. Therefore the formula needed for row 15 is =B12-B13.

6   Our final task is to copy the formulas in B12, B13 and B15 across the sheet.

Note: All of the money values in the sheet are shown in pence. It would be easier to show the larger numbers in rows 12, 13 and 15, in pounds. This can be done in two steps:

7   Divide by 100 to change pence into pounds.

8   Format the cells to currency to show the £ sign.

	A	B	C	D	E	F
12	Total sales	£25.75	£27.00	£12.25	£11.40	
13	Total costs	£20.60	£21.60	£8.82	£5.70	
14						
15	Weekly profit	£5.15	£5.40	£3.43	£5.70	

Question

A spreadsheet is used to help manage the stock in a car accessories shop. Part of this spreadsheet is shown below:

	A	B	C	D
1	Description	Unit Cost	Quantity	
2				
3	Cans of oil	6.50	40	260.00
4	Bottles of antifreeze	4.00	25	100.00
5	Tool kits	14.50	45	652.50
6	Car jacks	24.00	18	432.00
7				
8			Total value =	1444.50

a   Write out the formula in D8 that will work out the value shown.

   ....

b   Other than the cells containing a formula, give examples of two other forms of information that has been typed into the sheet.

   i   Type: ....   Cell address: ....

   ii   Type: ....   Cell address: ....

c   It has been decided to reduce the stock levels to £1000. Explain how the spreadsheet could be used to help do this.

   ....

   ....

d   Complete the sentences using words from the list given below:

   copied   C5   A1   formatted   D5   recalculated
   D8   A5   formula   what   if   bold   B3

   "The cells in columns B and D have been .... to display

   the numbers to 2 decimal places. The cell D3 contains a

   .... and this has been .... into cells D4, D5

   and D6. If the unit cost for the tool kits where to change in cell B5,

   this would change the values in .... and ...."

Computer graphics

Generating graphics on the computer has many different and important uses. Drawing and painting packages can be used by illustrators to create images, and games programmers use graphics extensively to produce fast and exciting animations. Many of the special effects seen on television have been generated through computer graphics, and computer aided design (CAD) is vital for many businesses (eg engineering, architecture, etc).

Painting packages

Painting programs such as *Paint®* which comes with *Windows®* are always popular. Paint programs are usually raster graphics packages where the image is held as a bitmap. The picture is made up of tiny picture elements called pixels (see page 13).

When you zoom into a bitmap image the edges are often jagged and it is not always easy to rescale the picture. Bitmap images take up a lot of computer memory as even the blank parts of the picture are stored.

Drawing packages

Drawing programs, like *Microsoft® Draw®*, use vector graphics. This means that the shapes which are drawn are stored in memory as a series of instructions. This makes them easy to rescale and they take up less memory.

Clipart

Many programs come with their own library of professionally prepared graphics for use in documents and publications. Both floppy disks and CDs can be purchased containing different clipart pictures.

Input devices used with drawing and painting packages are the mouse, scanners (digitisers) and graphics tablets (see pages 5 to 6).

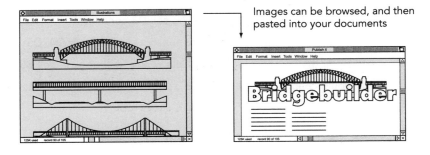

Images can be browsed, and then pasted into your documents

Computer aided design (CAD)

CAD packages are used by scientists, engineers and designers to design cars, roads, bridges, ships, waterways, circuit boards, computers, machinery, dams, chemical plants, oil rigs and buildings. The software needed is often complex and requires powerful computers to run it.

Computer aided design packages have many special features, including:

- adding measurements (dimensions) to the drawing

- allowing the designer to draw an object in two-dimensions (flat) and then having the software build and display a three-dimensional solid version of the design

- allowing the object being designed to be rotated and viewed from different angles

- 'suggesting' suitable materials for constructing the objects, eg materials with sufficient strength or flexibility

- calculating the stresses and strains that a structure will have to withstand and where necessary give warnings of designs that are not safe

- simulating and testing the finished design, eg where CAD is used to design an electronic circuit it can simulate the operation of the circuit.

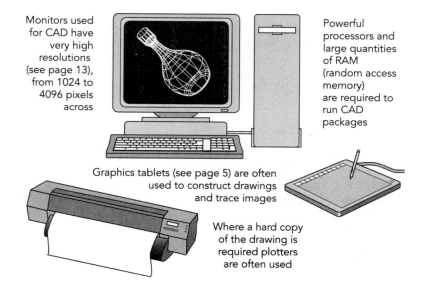

Monitors used for CAD have very high resolutions (see page 13), from 1024 to 4096 pixels across

Powerful processors and large quantities of RAM (random access memory) are required to run CAD packages

Graphics tablets (see page 5) are often used to construct drawings and trace images

Where a hard copy of the drawing is required plotters are often used

Using CAD software enables drawings to be done more quickly. Changes can be made without having to start the whole drawing again and parts of drawings which are needed more than once can be copied and then duplicated as many times as required. Many companies have large libraries of drawings held on disk which can be retrieved and modified very rapidly. Very fine detail can be achieved by zooming in on the drawing and many of the tedious tasks of hatching and shading areas can be done automatically by the computer.

Using a computer network, a number of designers can work on the same project at the same time and workers throughout the company, from the board room to the shop floor, can access drawings on their terminals to assist them with their work and decision making.

Computer aided design software is not just a drawing package. It can be sophisticated software that can calculate, from the dimensions of the drawing, the weight, strains and the stresses that the finished object will endure. In this way weakness in structures like bridges can be avoided. When using CAD software to design electronic circuits, the software can simulate voltages to test the circuit even before it has been constructed.

Computer aided manufacture (CAM)

Computer aided manufacture is a process of aiding production in manufacturing companies by using computers to operate machines. Some machines shape materials; three of the more common processes are latheing, milling and drilling:

| A lathed component | A milled component | A drilled component |

Other machines transport the goods between one process and the next, and computer-controlled robot arms may be involved in spraying paint or welding joints.

CAD/CAM

The most effective method of production is to design products using a computer aided design package and then pass instructions directly from this package to the machines able to manufacture the product. Data from the design software is translated into instructions for guiding the lathes, milling and drilling machines. The whole process is fully automated. The introduction of these systems into manufacturing industry have:

- increased production – machines do not need breaks or sleep

- dramatically reduced the numbers of workers

- reduced the demand for machine operators

- created the demand for skilled computer operators.

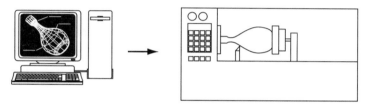

Product is designed on CAD system, the data is transferred to computer numeric control (CNC) machines, and the product manufactured with CAM

Questions

1 Explain the term CAD.

....

....

2 State three features/facilities you might expect to find on the drawing screen in a computer aided design package.

....

....

....

3 Give two differences between the type of monitor used to produce complex and detailed drawings in CAD and the monitor purchased for use on a home or school computer.

i ....

ii ....

Modelling and simulation packages

Modelling packages

Modelling is when a computer program attempts to represent a real situation. In order to do this, mathematical equations are used, but the accuracy of the computer model depends on how well the 'real' process is understood. Different values can be input to the model to investigate possible outcomes. A spreadsheet can be used as a modelling program.

Simulation packages

A simulation program is designed to predict the likely behaviour of a real-life system. The real-life situation is represented as a mathematical model in the computer program. Simulation packages include flight simulators and weather forecasting.

The illustration below shows how a modelling program could also be designed to assist in the construction of a flood protection scheme.

The computer model can experiment with different flood protection barriers of varying lengths, heights and positions to find the most effective and lowest cost protection system

The height of tides, the effects of air pressure and the effect of global warming on the sea level can be modelled by the computer and used as inputs to the program. The computer program can calculate the volume and flow of water based on these inputs

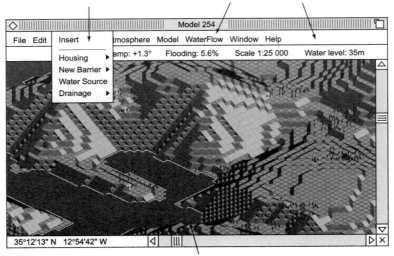

The land levels, natural barriers and water movements can be built into the model

Flight simulators can be purchased from a computer store for home PC computers. These test the ability of the user to fly an aeroplane including take-off, steady flight, navigation, flying stunts and landing using a joystick, keyboard or joypad.

A more serious use for the flight simulator is in the training of real pilots. Aircraft are expensive items, both to buy and fly. Learning to handle engine failure in zero visibility in the actual aircraft can be both a dangerous and costly exercise.

Modern flight simulators used for training pilots are full-size cockpits mounted on hydraulic arms to give a full range of movement. Computer screens are positioned in place of windows and these display lifelike images which change according to movement of the aircraft through the controls.

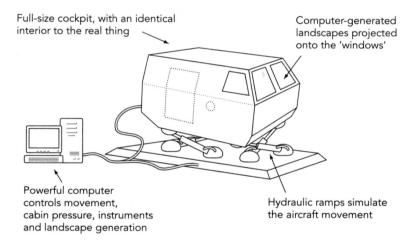

Full-size cockpit, with an identical interior to the real thing

Computer-generated landscapes projected onto the 'windows'

Powerful computer controls movement, cabin pressure, instruments and landscape generation

Hydraulic ramps simulate the aircraft movement

To be able to train a pilot in a lifelike simulator without leaving the ground can have a number of advantages. These include:

- the simulator is less expensive to operate than an actual aeroplane
- pilot training is not affected by weather conditions
- training in emergency situations can be safely given
- different conditions like night flying can be simulated
- practice can be give for take-off and landing at airports worldwide at the press of a button.

10 CD-ROMs and multimedia

Computer CD-ROMs (see page 23) are a relatively recent development and yet the number of discs now available is huge. Most microcomputers now have CD-ROM drives included as standard. CD-ROMs are 12 cm diameter discs which can hold 650 MB of data in the form of the following, or any mixture of them:

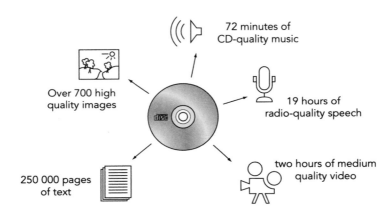

- 72 minutes of CD-quality music
- Over 700 high quality images
- 19 hours of radio-quality speech
- 250 000 pages of text
- two hours of medium quality video

Uses of CD-ROMs

One of the most important areas of use is in education and home entertainment where a wide range of discs are now available. Text and graphics from some CD-ROMs can be copied into the word processing software on the computer and then edited and printed. (Note: Care should be taken to ensure that copyright is not breached.)

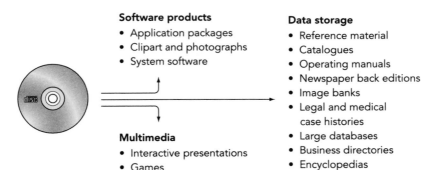

Software products
- Application packages
- Clipart and photographs
- System software

Multimedia
- Interactive presentations
- Games

Data storage
- Reference material
- Catalogues
- Operating manuals
- Newspaper back editions
- Image banks
- Legal and medical case histories
- Large databases
- Business directories
- Encyclopedias

CD-ROMs can hold a mixture of all these different item; because of this and the low cost of production (less than 50p each if producing 1000s) they have become very popular for distributing multimedia presentations.

Multimedia

Multimedia is the combination of text, images and sound in an interactive way where the viewer has some control over the delivery of information. When we watch a television programme, we have no control over what we watch, other than to change channels, or turn the television off.

In a multimedia presentation, however, the user has numerous options of which direction the program takes – we say that the program interacts with the user. It can be stopped, paused, restarted, back-tracked, and replayed at will.

Example of a CD-ROM for education and learning

A popular and well-known CD-ROM is the encyclopedia Microsoft® Encarta. The 1998 edition contains 30,000 articles with more than 12,000 photos and illustrations, 140 video clips and animations and over 4000 music and audio clips.

Question

One type of information stored on a CD-ROM is text. Give two other types of information that can be stored on a CD-ROM.

i ....

....

....

ii ....

....

....

11 Data logging

Data logging can be defined as the capture and storage of data for use at a later time. Sensors are used to input the data which is stored in memory. This data can then be displayed in graphs and tables, passed to a spreadsheet program for analysis, printed and saved on computer disk. Data logging is particularly important in scientific experiments.

Sensors

Almost all physical properties can be measured with sensors. There are sensors to measure light, heat, sound, movement, pressure, strains and stresses in materials, acidity and humidity. Some of the more common sensors are described in detail in the input devices section (see pages 11 and 12).

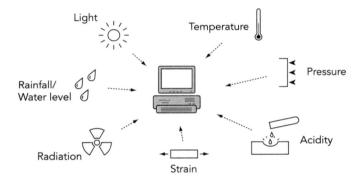

When an experiment is taking place in the laboratory it is possible to link sensors directly through their control boxes to the computer. If we wish to record data out in the field, equipment would be needed that could measure and store data until the unit is brought to a computer and the data downloaded. Where the recording was taking place would determine how robust the data logging equipment would have to be. For example, if it was recording a river height or the pH level, it would have to be waterproof. In chemical plants the equipment might have to be resistant to acids and alkalis. Data logging equipment in a satellite would need to work in a vacuum and extremes of temperature.

Why use data logging equipment for experiments?

There are a number of advantages in using data logging in experiments. These include:

- Data loggers can record measurements with great accuracy.

- Sometimes the very act of taking a reading may interfere with the experiment, eg inserting a thermometer in a liquid may cool the liquid a fraction and also allow heat to escape through a lid. Sensors can be sealed inside the equipment.

- Data loggers can collect data measurements over very short or very long periods of time. For example, equipment could record and process hundreds of measurements during a chemical reaction lasting less than a second or it could be set to record the growth of a plant by taking measurements every hour, day and night, for months or even years.

- Data logging equipment can work reliably and consistently for long periods of time. People would need to take breaks to eat and sleep, and when tired their efficiency may be reduced.

- Data loggers can operate in environments which would be hostile to people. Equipment can be designed to operate in orbiting satellites, the depths of the oceans, deserts, or the Arctic.

Analogue and digital

A digital signal consists of pulses of electricity passing along a wire or track of a circuit board. At any point in the signal there are only two states, either a pulse of electricity is present or there is no pulse. There is no in-between state.

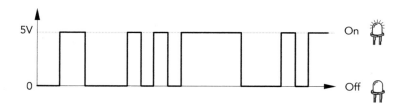

Computers operate using digital signals and all the data and program instructions are coded with different combinations of '1s' and '0s'.

Many sensors which are used to input data into computers produce analogue signals. Take, for example, a light-dependent resistor (LDR) sensor which reacts to the amount of light falling on it. The resistance to the flow of electricity through the device gets less as the light becomes brighter.

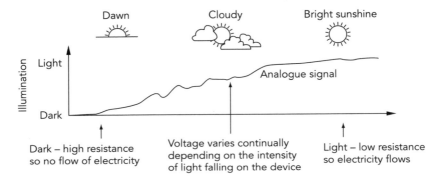

Because computers only work with digital signals, the analogue signals from the sensor must be converted to digital signals. This is done by an electronic device called an 'analogue to digital converter' (or 'A to D converter' for short). The varying voltage of the analogue signal is converted into pulses.

Sometimes it is necessary to reverse this process and take the digital signal from the computer to an output device that needs an analogue signal. In this case a 'digital to analogue converter' (or 'D to A converter') is used.

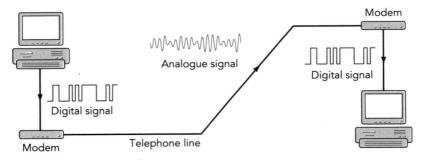

For example, the audio signal that travels along the telephone wire is analogue. A modem (see page 83) is both an 'A to D converter' and a 'D to A converter'. When connecting a computer to the Internet using telephone cables, the modem converts the incoming signals to digital for the computer and the outgoing signals from the computer to analogue to travel along the wires.

Question

In the science experiment shown on the right the beaker contains a clear liquid. When a second substance is added to the beaker the two react and the contents of the beaker turn cloudy thus preventing the light passing through.

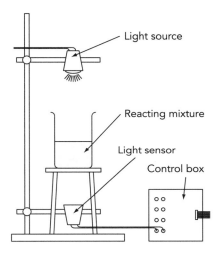

a What electronic component might be used as the light sensor?

....

....

....

b Would the output from the light sensor be an analogue or a digital signal?

....

c What form of signal does the computer require in order to process data – analogue or digital?

....

d Give two reasons why this reaction might be best monitored using the data logging equipment shown.

....

....

....

....

e If instead of the liquid in the beaker going cloudy, the reaction caused the temperature of the liquid to increase, say how you might modify the experiment to monitor this.

....

....

....

12 Computer control

Computers are now used to control the operation of many machines and everyday objects. The instructions contained in the computer program send signals out of the computer to devices like switches and motors which make the machine operate in the correct way.

Example of a control program

One programming language used to control the movements of a simple object is Logo. This language was designed for pupils in junior schools and can make a mechanical 'turtle' move around the floor on a sheet of paper (or an image on screen). The turtle has a pen which can be lowered onto the paper so that a trail is left as the turtle moves across the paper. The table below shows some of the instructions from Logo:

FORWARD n	Move 'n' steps forward
BACKWARD n	Move 'n' steps backward
RIGHT d	Turn 'd' degrees to the right
LEFT d	Turn 'd' degrees to the left
PENUP	Lift the pen off the paper
PENDOWN	Lower the pen down onto the paper

To draw a square (size 50 units) and a hexagon (size 30 units) on the paper we would program in the following instructions:

Square	**Hexagon** (6 sides)
PENDOWN	PENDOWN
FORWARD 50	FORWARD 30
RIGHT 90	RIGHT 60
FORWARD 50	FORWARD 30
RIGHT 90	RIGHT 60
FORWARD 50	FORWARD 30
RIGHT 90	RIGHT 60
FORWARD 50	FORWARD 30
PENUP	RIGHT 60
	FORWARD 30
	RIGHT 60
	FORWARD 30
	PENUP

These short programs contain several sets of repeated instructions. The program code can be shortened by using another Logo instruction:

REPEAT x [instruction]

This repeats the instructions in the brackets 'x' times.

The programs could now be written as shown below:

Square

```
PENDOWN
REPEAT 4 [FORWARD 50 RIGHT 90]
PENUP
```

Hexagon

```
PENDOWN
REPEAT 6 [FORWARD 30 RIGHT 60]
PENUP
```

When a computer is used to control machines it is often necessary to input data from both the machines and the surrounding environment. The sorts of input and output devices associated with computer control are illustrated below (more detail on these devices is given on pages 4 to 18):

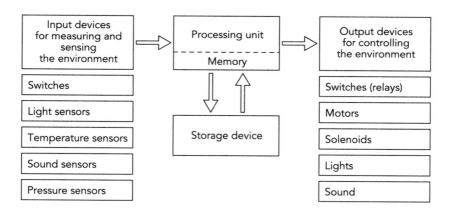

Feedback

Feedback is a term used in computer control when data input from a sensor causes the control program to make changes by sending signals to output devices. These changes are then recorded by the input sensor and data signals sent back to the computer. This process forms a loop as illustrated in the example below:

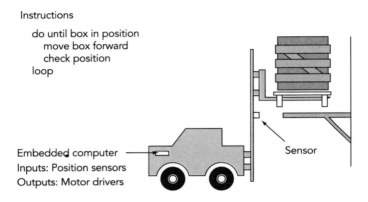

Instructions

    do until box in position
      move box forward
      check position
    loop

Embedded computer
Inputs: Position sensors
Outputs: Motor drivers

Sensor

Machine putting a box onto a shelf in a warehouse

Embedded computers

When a computer is used to control a machine, the computer circuit board is installed inside the machine. The input sensors and output control devices are then connected to these circuits. This is an embedded computer. The input/output devices that we are most familiar with – the keyboard, mouse, monitor and disk drive – are not required.

The computer control program is written using a 'normal' computer and 'downloaded' into the embedded computer. The software program is stored in a ROM (Read Only Memory) chip and activates when the machine is switched on.

Why use computers for control?

- Although the cost of computerised machines in factories is high, the operating costs are low in comparison to wages for people doing the job.
- Computers work without the need for breaks and sleep.
- The quality of output from the machine is consistent.
- Machines can handle very heavy work or very precise tasks.
- Machines can work in places that are uncomfortable or hostile for people.
- Computers process data very quickly and so the machines can operate faster.
- Computers can operate the machines with data from a range of sources.

Applications

Washing machines

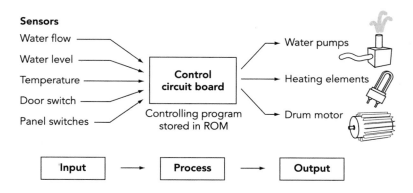

Inputs: Water flow sensors, water level sensors, temperature sensors, panel switches, door open switch, spin speed selector.

Process: Stored programs for different wash cycles, eg woollens, cotton, etc. Each program controls the water temperature and level, and the timing and sequence of the wash, rinse and spin cycles.

Outputs: Switches to operate water pumps and valves, water heaters and the drum motor.

Microwave oven

Inputs: Switches from the key pad, door closed sensor.

Process: Mainly timing processes but also sequences of microwave and grill functions.

Outputs: Switches to control grill and microwave power settings, inside light and buzzer.

Toys

Inputs: Usually switches, sometimes sound or light activated.

Process: Various, depending on the toy.

Outputs: Lights, sound, switching motors, LCD screens.

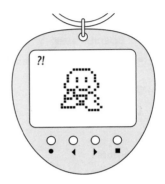

Central heating controllers

Inputs: Switches on key pad.

Process: Mainly timing functions, storing several on/off settings for each day.

Outputs: Switches to turn the boiler on/off, to operate pumps and solenoids to control valves in the pipes.

Trials have been made using more sophisticated controllers that monitor whether a room is in use and switch off the heating in unused rooms. These controllers have the facility to 'learn' and can establish patterns of movement in the house. For example, a person goes to bed at around 10:30 pm each night then the controller will detect this and switch the heating on in the bedroom just before this time.

Watches

Inputs: Push button switches.

Process: Date, day, time, timer, alarm and stopwatch facilities.

Outputs: LCD screen or hour and minute hands and alarm beeper.

Burglar alarms

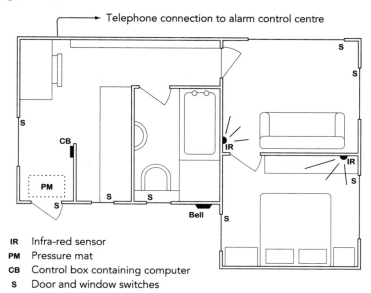

Telephone connection to alarm control centre

IR Infra-red sensor
PM Pressure mat
CB Control box containing computer
S   Door and window switches

Inputs: Switches on windows and doors, pressure pads under carpets
            and infra-red sensors in rooms and hallways.

Process: Trigger the alarm instantly from window switches and pressure
            pads, timer to allow entry via the door to switch off the alarm
            circuits.

Outputs: Internal buzzer and siren, outside bell and lights, connection to
            police station/security control room over telephone line.

Video recorders

Inputs: Switches on the control panel, infra-red detector for remote key
            pad, switches to detect whether the video tape is in the machine
            and the tape's recording/play back time.

Process: Timer and clock for switching the recorder on/off, memory to
            hold different recording dates and times, automatic scanning to
            find television channels.

Outputs: LCD display on front panel, switches to operate video tape drive
            motors.

Camera

Inputs: Light sensor, push buttons, film speed sensor, battery power and end of film sensor.

Process: Calculate light level and adjust shutter speed and aperture (size of hole allowing light in) according to film speed. Focus the lens to produce a sharp image. Activate motor to wind film on and draw back shutter for the next picture. Activate flash if necessary.

Outputs: Shutter release switch, motor on/off switch, flash.

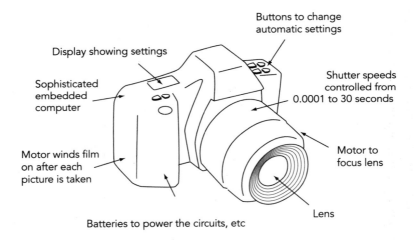

Buttons to change automatic settings

Display showing settings

Sophisticated embedded computer

Shutter speeds controlled from 0.0001 to 30 seconds

Motor winds film on after each picture is taken

Motor to focus lens

Batteries to power the circuits, etc

Lens

Robotic arm

Inputs: Movement co-ordinates entered at a keyboard or memorised as a skilled worker guides the arm in a learning process, pressure sensors, switches.

Process: Arm follows a pattern of movements held in memory. Switches operate the tools, eg spray painting car bodies on a car manufacturing production line. Sensors on the arm detect and feedback information on its position in relation to the job.

Outputs: Switches to control movement (electric motors, pneumatic valves or hydraulic pumps). Switches to operate the tools being used by the arm.

Questions

1 A car park has automatic entry and exit barriers to allow cars in and out. The computer program that controls these barriers contains a number of variables (memory locations storing data):

Variable	Description
cars_start	the number of cars in the car park at the beginning of the day
cars_in	the number of cars entering the car park
cars_out	the number of cars leaving the car park
max_cars	the maximum number of car parking spaces available

Each time a car enters the car park the number in 'cars_in' increments (goes up) by one. As a car leaves the number in 'cars_out' increments by one.

a Another variable called 'total_cars' is used to hold the total number of cars in the car park at any one time. Show how this can be calculated from the variables above.

....

b Using the variable 'total_cars', which of the following lines of code would test to see if the entrance barrier should be opened?

☐ If total_cars < max_cars
☐ If total_cars > cars_out
☐ If cars_in - cars_out = zero
☐ If max_cars <cars_start

< less than
> greater than

c A light beam was used to detect cars entering the car park. As the car broke the beam, a signal was passed to the computer from the light sensor. It was soon found that pedestrians taking a short-cut into the car park through the barrier were triggering the sensor. Describe a better way of detecting the cars entering.

....

....

....

....

d It is decided to make all the automatic car park data available on an Internet site so that people could check which car parks were full before setting out from home. What additional data from the car park could be added to help the driver?

....

....

....

2 The illustration below shows the storage racks in a warehouse. A computer-controlled forklift truck delivers boxes to the racks according to a set of programmed instructions.

a Five packages have been placed on the shelves in order. The instructions for the first two packages are given below. Complete the instructions for the other three packages.

Package 1   F2,1   (Forward 2 racks, level 1 shelf)
Package 2   B1,3   (Back 1 rack, level 3 shelf)
Package 3   ....
Package 4   ....
Package 5   ....

b How would it be possible for the computer program controlling the truck to have an extra check on its position in the warehouse?

....

....

....

....

A vital part of Information Technology is for computers to send data to other computers, peripherals and control devices. There are a number of ways in which this data can travel:

With cables

Wire cables

Signal carrying core

Twisted pairs

+ Cheap and easy to use
− Signal needs boosting over long distances

Wire braid protects from interference

Co-axial cable

Fibre optic cable

+ Can carry many signals at the same time
+ Free from electrical interference
+ Data is secure
+ Does not suffer from corrosion
− Equipment and cables are expensive

Thin glass fibre

A light beam travels through the fibre, carrying the digital signal

Protective sheaths

Without cables

Microwave

+ Secure data communication between remote sites
− Direct line of sight required

Infra-red

+ Freedom of movement for the machine
− Must have direct line of sight
− May be affected by strong sunlight

Satellite

+ Communication between continents
− Expensive to put satellites in orbit

Satellites use a narrow, highly directional beam capable of many simultaneous transmissions. They need to be in an orbit such that its position above the Earth does not change

Local Area Networks (LANs)

Computer systems are networked when they are linked together. This linking can be through wire cables, fibre optic cables, microwave links or satellite. When computer systems are linked on the same site, eg a school, this is called a Local Area Network (LAN).

File server

A file server is a powerful computer which holds the software to run the network. It also holds the shared resources of the network like the users' files, software packages and printer queues.

The advantages of using a network computer are:

- Printers can be shared: individual stations do not need their own printer. When they print the data is stored in a queue on the file server. The data is then passed to the printer in turn.

- Programs can be shared: software packages are stored on the file server and downloaded to stations as requested.

- Data can be shared: database files stored in the file server are available to users around the network; data from CD-ROMs can also be shared.

- Users can communicate with others on the network, sending messages and sharing files.

Network topology

Network topology is the name given to the way in which the computers are connected in the network. Computers can be connected in a bus, star or ring network structure:

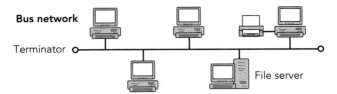

Bus network

Terminator

File server

+ Easy and inexpensive to install (least amount of cable required)
− If the main cable fails, all the computers will be affected
− Performance of the network slows down with more users

Star network

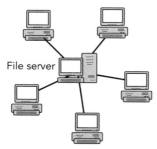

File server

Ring network

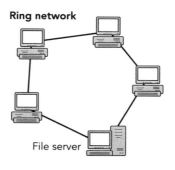

File server

+ Steady high performance, affected less by how many other computers on the network are being used
+ A cable failure does not affect other users
− Uses a lot of cables which is expensive
− Requires a 'hub' box at the file server to control all the cables

+ Data traffic between stations on the network is fast as it flows in one direction only
− If the cable fails, all the stations are affected

When using a computer on a network it is necessary to 'log on' using a user name and password. The person responsible for looking after the network is called the network manager. They can give each user access to the particular programs they need.

Wide Area Networks (WANs)

When computers are linked over larger geographical areas they form a Wide Area Network. An example of a Wide Area Network is the Internet which allows computer users to link to other computers around the world, often for the price of a local phone call. To enable a computer to send and receive data using the telephone line, a modem is required.

Modem

The word 'modem' is short for MOdulator DEModulator. Modems convert the digital signals in the computer to audio tones which can travel across the telephone system. It also converts incoming signals back into a digital form. The speed at which modems can transmit and receive data varies. The faster the modem, the quicker data transfers will be and lower telephone charges will result. A typical speed for an efficient Internet modem is 56 kbps (kilobits per second). Each character on the keyboard is made up of a code of eight bits. This means a modem working at this speed could receive over 6000 characters in a second.

ISDN (Integrated Services Digital Network)

ISDN lines are now being installed in businesses, schools and homes. These are digital lines which mean that computers can link directly to each other without the need for a modem. ISDN lines provide faster data transfer rates than ordinary telephone lines and transmissions are also more error free. Typical data transfer speeds are 56 kbps.

Packet switching

Data travels around the Internet along telephone lines, network cables, fibre optic cables, and radio and satellite links. The data is sent as a packet with the destination address at the front of the message. As each packet of data travels along the network it meets nodes (connection points) consisting of powerful mini- and mainframe computers. These computers re-route the packet towards its destination address. Larger quantities of data being sent are split into smaller packets, each with the destination address, and may travel on different routes across the network before being reassembled again in the correct order at the destination.

O Point of Presence (PoP) or network node

Internet

The Internet is a huge international network made up of many smaller networks linked together like a spider's web. It started as a 'self-healing' communication system for the US government in case of nuclear disaster. It was then taken up by the academic community to exchange research material. It grew to include business and personal networks and is now a vast network spanning the globe.

The Internet provides a vast range of information resources which can be accessed from your school or home computer. This information can be placed onto the Web by the millions of different users around the world without any form of regulation. This means that care must be taken when viewing different sites. Some material is very exact, detailed and informative; other sources may hold inaccurate information, and some sites hold quite offensive material.

Accessing the Internet

All that is required to use the Internet is:

- a computer
- a modem or ISDN connection
- communications software
- access to a local PoP (Point of Presence).

There are many organisations providing the link, or point of presence, where you dial in over the telephone (normally a local call) to make your connection to the Internet. These organisations, known as Internet Service providers (ISP), supply the communications software and charge a small monthly subscription. Some major ISPs include BT Campusworld, Compuserve, Demon Internet, UK Online and AOL. In order to explore and retrieve information a browser in required. Two popular browsers are Netscape Navigator and Microsoft₀ Internet Explorer₀.

Email

Email, or electronic mail, is a way of sending messages, data, files or graphics to other users on the network. Subscribers to the Internet are given an email address, eg info@pearson.co.uk.

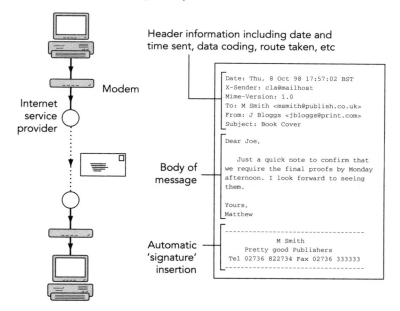

Email allows messages to be sent to anyone on the network, even on the other side of the world, for the price of the local phone call. When messages arrive at their destination, often only minutes after they have been sent, they are stored in a mailbox. When the person receiving the message connects to the network, they are informed of incoming mail waiting to be read. After reading this mail the user can:

- delete the message
- file the message by storing it on disk
- send back a reply
- forward the message on to one or more other people.

Electronic bulletin boards

Electronic bulletin boards are an electronic form of a notice-board. When users on the network visit the bulletin board site they can read messages or leave their own for other to read. It is also possible to collect software programs from bulletin board areas. Usenet is one example of a bulletin board.

The usenet is a collection of newsgroups each on a single theme such as football, cooking or books. Each newsgroup contains postings from people, some providing information, some requesting information. When new announcements are made or queries asked, an ongoing discussion may start in the newsgroup. Nearly all usenet newsgroups have FAQs (frequently asked questions) sections which hold answers to the most commonly asked questions. It is considered polite (or correct 'netiquette') for new users to read this information first before asking questions.

World Wide Web (www)

The World Wide Web is what draws most people onto the 'Net'. The www allows users to publish multimedia pages, containing text, graphics, sound and video information for users of the Net to view. An example of a Web site address is: http://www.pearson.co.uk/education/

Businesses, schools and individuals can make their own Web site pages incorporating text, graphics, digital sound and video. This can be done using PC software like Microsoft FrontPage98. Different Web pages can be linked using hypertext hotlinks, in other words new pages are selected by clicking with the mouse on the linking text or graphics. Each Web site on the Internet has a unique address, starting with the letters http:// (Hyper-Text Transfer Protocol). These Web addresses are termed URL (Uniform Resource Locator).

What is available on the Internet?

'Surfing', 'cruising' or 'browsing' the Net are terms used for accessing the Internet. Information on thousands of different topics can be shared through user groups, Web pages and electronic bulletin boards. These include:

- art
- banks
- books
- business
- computers
- education
- entertainment
- exhibitions
- films
- food and drink
- games
- health
- hobbies
- museums
- music
- nature
- politics
- radio
- real estate
- religion
- science
- shopping
- sport
- transport
- travel
- universities
- weather

Questions

1 When using a computer on a Local Area Network explain:

a why is it necessary to have a password?

....

b why passwords should be changed regularly?

....

c why when a user changes their password they are asked to type in the new password, and then type it in again?

....

2 Complete the following sentences by choosing the correct words from the list below:

WAN   modem   OCR   email   word processor   MAN   Byte
model   formatting   printer   LAN   virus

"A .... connects the computers in a school. Students can

also access the school's computers from home using a ....

The school has access to the Internet which is a .... , and

students each send messages using ...."

3 The diagram below shows the layout of a network used in a veterinary practice. A workstation and printer is located in every consulting room.

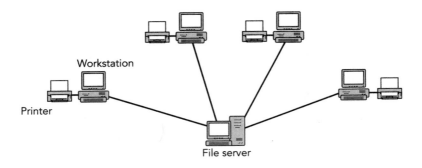

Workstation

Printer

File server

a What type of network topology (structure) is used in this LAN?

   ....

b Give two advantages of having a network instead of stand-alone machines in each consulting room.

   ....

   ....

It is decided to join all the veterinary practices in the county to form a Wide Area Network (WAN).

c What extra device would be needed to join the LAN to a WAN?

   ....

d What is the function of this device?

   ....

e What security problems might arise for the surgery by linking up to the WAN?

   ....

Types of file structure

There are four ways in which data files can be structured on a computer disk. These are as follows:

Sample records from a file:

Customer number	Name
1048	Brown
1051	Carter
1054	Cross
1052	Chesterton
1049	Bull
1050	Butler

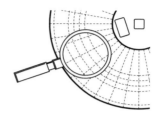

Serial

The data items or records that make up the file are placed one after the other, in no particular order.

1051 Carter	1048 Brown	1054 Cross	1049 Bull	1055...

Sequential

If a file has a sequential structure the records are placed one after the other, just like the serial structure, but the records are in order of their key fields.

1048 Brown	1049 Bull	1050 Butler	1051 Carter	1052...

Indexed sequential

The records are arranged one after the other in sequence of their key field and an index is also kept of the key field and the address on the disk where the record is to be found. The index is usually stored with the records and transferred to memory (RAM) when the file is used.

Key field	Disk address
1048	237
1049	238
1050	239
...	...

1048 Brown	1049 Bull	1050 Butler	1051 Carter	1052...

Random

When records in a file are stored with a random structure (also known as direct access), the address on the disk for each record is calculated from the key field. This process of calculating the address is known as hashing and the sequence of actions done by the computer program is known as a hashing algorithm.

	1051 Carter			
1049 Bull			1050 Butler	
		1052 Chesterton		1048 Brown

One type of hashing algorithm, the division and remainder method, is shown below:

Suppose the key field for a record was five digits long and the number of memory locations available for storing the data was about 1000. A suitable prime number is chosen, slightly less than the number of memory locations available. In this case the prime number could be 997.

> The address of a record with a key field of 12345 would be:
>
> $$\frac{12345}{997} = 12 \text{ remainder } 381$$
>
> The record address becomes 381 on the disk.
>
> If two or more records have the same address, then the second record can be placed either in the next available space or in a reserved overflow area of the disk.

Hit rate

The hit rate is a measure of how many data items (or records in a database) are accessed during the operation of the program. It is calculated by:

$$\text{Hit rate} = \frac{\text{Number accessed}}{\text{Total number}} \times 100$$

The hit rate is expressed as a percentage.

High 'hit rate': When a company payroll program runs, 349 records are accessed out of a total of 352 records. The hit rate is:

$$\text{Hit rate} = \frac{\text{Number accessed}}{\text{Total number}} \times 100 = \frac{349}{352} \times 100 = 99\%$$

Sequential files are good for high hit rate applications.

Low 'hit rate': If the customer services department received an average of 21 calls from customers each day from a customer base of 7000, then the hit rate is:

$$\text{Hit rate} = \frac{\text{Number accessed}}{\text{Total number}} \times 100 = \frac{21}{7000} \times 100 = 0.3\%$$

Random files are good for low hit rate applications.

Uses for the different file structures:

Type	Example of use
Serial	A shop might use a serial file to record sales by customers during the course of a day. As each purchase is made, details of the sale are added (appended) to the end of the file.
Sequential	When a serial file containing customer sales is used to update the main customer record file (master file) the records must first be sorted into order. It then becomes a sequential file.
Indexed sequential	These files are good for low and high 'hit rate' applications. Keeping a file for staff records might use indexed sequential files. Individual records can be retrieved quickly using the index and all the records can be accessed when the payroll is run each month.
Random	A random (or direct access) structure is often used with large files that have low hit rates. A computerised school library might use a random file to access details of books borrowed by scanning a bar code.

Questions

1 A computerised theatre booking system uses realtime processing. The software stores details of seat bookings using random (direct) access records. Explain the difference between random and serial access.

....

....

2 A file contains 1200 records. Calculate the hit rate percentage for the file when:

a 24 records are accessed during a session

....

b 900 records are accessed during a session.

....

15 Flow charts

Flow charts are used to illustrate processes and operations in computers. There are a number of different types of flow chart, this book looks at two sorts: program flow charts and system flow charts.

Program flow charts

These are used to show the operations involved in a computer program. Different symbols are used to represent particular operations. Flow charts can be constructed before the program instructions are written to help the programmer or they can be constructed afterwards to help document the program. Documentation is important to help other users to understand how the program works so that future maintenance can take place.

Symbol	Description	Example
	Connector Used when a flow chart continues on the next page	bottom of first page / top of second page
	Terminator Used for 'start' and 'stop'	STOP
	Input/output Used to show input and output of data	Read name
	Decision Used to illustrate different paths being taken based on decisions. Decision boxes can have more than two exits	Is N>10? No Yes
	Process Used to represent a sequence of instructions or operations not involving a decision	Initialise variables
	Subroutine Used to indicate a sequence of instructions which will have its own flow chart elsewhere	Validate check digit

Example of a program flow chart

The following flow chart illustrates graphically the sequence of control instructions required to open a security door. A numeric keypad with a pass code of '1324' will unlock the door but if more than three wrong codes are entered an alarm will be triggered.

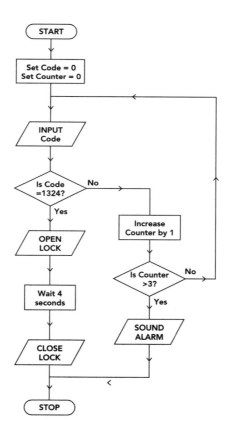

System flow charts

System flow charts are used to show how data in a computer system is processed. It does not involve the complex detail of the program instructions (which are represented by the program flow chart) but is a broad view of the system operation.

Symbol	Description	Example
	Process Represents a series of instructions to perform an operation. (This box could represent a whole program flowchart.)	Update files
	Sort Sort data or records in a file	Sort records
	Disk file Data file stored on magnetic disk	Master file
	Magnetic tape Data stored on magnetic tape	Back-up customer records
Small document Large document	**Document** Symbol for a printed document output from the system	Pay slips
	Keyboard Manual input through the keyboard	

Task: Run a payroll program and print the payslips.

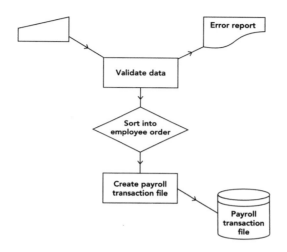

Details of the hours worked and overtime done are entered for each employee

The data entered is validated and sorted into employee number order before being saved to a payroll transaction file

The payroll transaction file is merged with the master file and the updated details are stored in a new master file

Details in the master file, such as total tax paid, require updating each month. Reports and payslips are printed

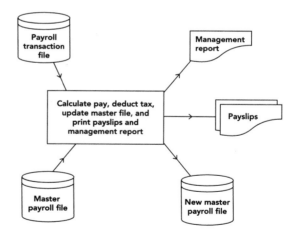

Data flow diagrams (DFD)

These diagrams show how a procedure or operation takes place with reference to the flow of data. This is often a useful illustration to include in the Communicating and Handling Information GCSE coursework project to show the way data is processed.

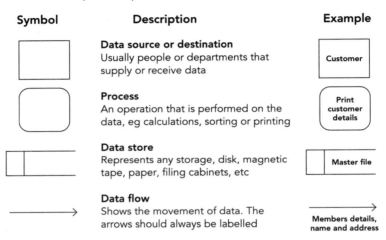

Symbol	Description	Example
	Data source or destination Usually people or departments that supply or receive data	Customer
	Process An operation that is performed on the data, eg calculations, sorting or printing	Print customer details
	Data store Represents any storage, disk, magnetic tape, paper, filing cabinets, etc	Master file
	Data flow Shows the movement of data. The arrows should always be labelled	Members details, name and address

Example of a data flow diagram

A customer sends off an order to a mail order company for goods. The company checks the order and payment when it arrives and then passes the order for processing. A 'picking list' is printed for the warehouse where the goods are packed and despatched to the customer. Details of the order are recorded in a 'customers file' and an invoice is despatched. The stock levels in the stock file are adjusted as the order is being processed.

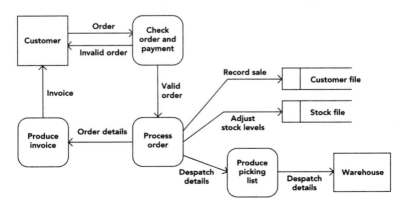

16 System design and development

GCSE IT projects and coursework

When we set out to use Information Technology to assist with a particular task we follow a structured series of processes. The stages in this series are similar whether carried out by a team of programmers for a company or a student doing a coursework project for their GCSE. No one can agree on a precise number of stages but the general pattern is as follows:

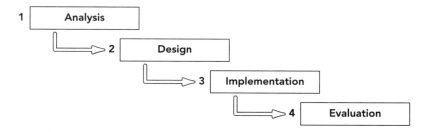

These two additional stages must also be included, either as separate stages, or sometimes they are included in the stage shown above:

For GCSE coursework you are required to investigate how IT could assist in a task or process. This will involve using one or more software packages that you know and the project may involve communicating and handling information, modelling, simulations, measurement, control or a mixture of these.

Each of the examination boards have slightly different coursework requirements in terms of the number of projects and the precise structure for presenting the work for marking.

Below are some guidance notes showing what may be included at each of the four stages of the system design. Documentation and testing have been included as parts of the main four stages:

Analysis

☐ Identify a task which will make sensible use of the IT tools

☐ Gather information about the task, eg show how it is currently done without the aid of a computer

☐ Define the problem

☐ Who are the potential users? Gather their views. Use a questionnaire or interview

☐ Produce a design specification to include all aspects of the task – include resource requirements

☐ What are the limitations of the potential users? Would they be able to manage your proposed system?

☐ What are the limitations imposed by the resources available – equipment, software packages and peripherals?

☐ Outline the objectives for the project

☐ Specify the data sources required for the task

☐ Other:

Design

☐ Look at a range of different solutions using different methods and software packages

☐ Consider the computer versus the non-computer solution and the effect of resources on the chosen design

☐ Choose one solution and justify the choice

☐ Show with system flow charts, data flow diagrams and block diagrams how the proposed solution will operate

☐ Ensure that the chosen design proposal matches the requirements of the potential users

☐ Describe the structure and quantity of input data required and the output from the system

- [ ] Show the design of forms, reports and queries that might be used in the system
- [ ] Explain if validation and verification of data is required/used in the solution
- [ ] Design a comprehensive test strategy for the system
- [ ] Other:

Implementation

- [ ] Show the use of the software packages and document some of the features used
- [ ] State how the solution works and use diagrams to illustrate this
- [ ] Ensure the results you produce match the design section
- [ ] Produce documentation for the user giving instruction on using the program, resource requirements and a troubleshooting guide
- [ ] Test your solution following the test strategy stated in the design section, and produce the evidence of testing
- [ ] Other:

Evaluation

- [ ] Compare the final solution with the design objectives set out in the analysis section
- [ ] Test results from your solution may be given here or in the implementation section
- [ ] Have your solution tested *in situ* doing the real task as set out in the analysis
- [ ] Document the opinions of other users testing and using your solution
- [ ] State the improvements made to the program as a result of testing
- [ ] State any enhancements and improvements that could be implemented
- [ ] Other:

Project work

A large part of the GCSE IT course involves project work. The notes below offer some further ideas that may help you to tackle this work.

Your report write-up should be word processed and it looks neatest if the same clear font is used throughout the report. Footers can be used to add page numbers to the report and a content page can be inserted at the front showing each section and its page number. A title page can also be added to enhance the presentation of the report. This should have the title, your name and your candidate number on it, but don't spend too long on this as it is unlikely to gain you extra marks.

The different examination boards give guidance in their syllabus as to how long (how many pages) they recommend the coursework project should be. It is possible to include extra material by placing it at the end of the project in an appendix section. This section could contain:

for communicating and handling information projects

- additional evidence from your investigation and analysis of the problem
- forms that you used to collect data (data capture forms)
- printouts of different forms created (eg in a database) to input data
- a printout of the data entered into the system
- your testing strategy and further printouts to show evidence that the system works
- evidence of different report outputs
- provide documentation for others to use your solution

for controlling, measuring and modelling projects

- as above but photographs or 'screen dumps' may be necessary as evidence instead of printouts.

Question

When a new piece of software is developed for a computer system, documentation in the form of a 'User Guide' should also be provided. State three topics which should be included in this guide.

....

....

17 Applications of IT

Computers are now used in almost every aspect of daily life. The examples that follow show a range of uses and illustrate some of the input, output and processing functions involved.

Computers in shops

It is important for shops to know how much stock to hold. Too much stock will take up valuable space, is costly and the shop runs the risk of products not being sold before their 'sell-by' date. Too little stock and customers will be unhappy when they cannot buy what they need. In larger stores and supermarkets the control of stock by constantly monitoring the sales is done by EPOS (Electronic Point of Sale) terminals – ie the checkout.

Bar codes

Each product has a bar code which represents the product's number. When the product is purchased, the scanner reads the black and white lines of the bar code to identify the product. The bar code number is passed to the computer which holds details of all the products in a large data file. An itemised receipt for the customer is produced, and the records are adjusted in the stock file.

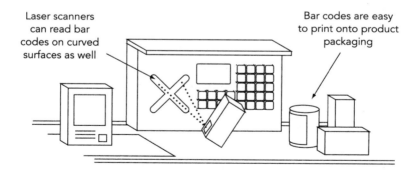

Laser scanners can read bar codes on curved surfaces as well

Bar codes are easy to print onto product packaging

Bar codes being laser scanned at a checkout till

The advantages of using an EPOS system for the customer include:

- much faster service at the checkout till – without a scanner the number on each item would need to be keyed in by the shop assistant
- scanning the goods gives greater accuracy than keying product numbers
- an itemised receipt describes the purchase and shows the price
- the computerised system makes multibuys easy to operate, eg 'Buy two, get a third free'
- goods are more likely to be fresh as the system improves stock control.

The advantages of using an EPOS system for the store manager include:

- customers pass through the checkouts more quickly and with less errors being made by the assistants
- goods in the shop do not have to be individually priced: only the edge of shelf price label needs to match the price in the computer
- the control of stock is fully automated: as each product passes through the checkout the level of stock is adjusted
- more efficient stock control means less stock needs to be kept, thus saving on both space and money
- as all the sales are monitored the managers can monitor the demand at the checkouts and ensure the correct staffing level.

Stock control

The manager of the store determines the minimum amount of stock for each product in the store. For example, this might be 200 cans of peas. As each tin of peas is purchased the number in stock is reduced by 1. When the number in stock falls below the minimum stock level (in this case 200), a message to reorder more cans is sent by the computer to the suppliers. If the shop is part of a group of shops, then the message is sent to the head office where all the orders are collated and dispatched to the suppliers.

The future

The large supermarket chains are constantly striving to improve their services to customers ahead of their competitors. New ideas based on Information Technology are being trialled including:

- allowing customers to scan the product bar codes themselves
- home shopping where the order is sent via the Internet to the local store where the goods are selected and packed.

Computers in banks and building societies

Banks were one of the first organisations to use computers. Introduced in the 1950s, computers were well established by the mid-1960s for tasks like processing cheques, calculating interest and keeping customers' accounts.

Processing cheques

Each day in Britain millions of cheques are cashed. Without computers this would not be possible and the financial world would grind to a halt. The key to processing so much data lies in the coded characters at the bottom of the cheque which are printed using an ink containing magnetic particles.

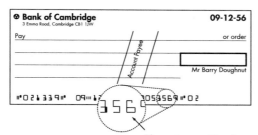

Characters written in magnetic ink

When the cheque is sent for processing, four sets of 'magnetic ink' numbers are required. These are:

1. the customer's account code – every customer is given a unique account number

2. the sort code – every branch of every bank or building society has their own sort code

3. the number of the cheque – within a book of cheques each cheque is numbered in sequence

4. the amount the cheque is made out for (added when the cheque is presented to a bank or building society for payment).

Using a recording head similar to that on a tape recorder, the numbers can be read into the computer at great speed (3000 cheques per minute). This input process is called MICR (magnetic ink character recognition). Using magnetic ink makes the cheques more difficult to forge and reading the cheque numbers is unaffected by scribbling over the characters.

ATMs (Automatic Teller Machines)

Obtaining cash at any time of the day or night from a cash dispenser (the ATM) is often more convenient than visiting the bank or building society. Also in recent years many employers have moved away from paying their workers in cash. Instead they transfer funds directly through to the workers' accounts so the need for these cash dispensers has grown.

To obtain cash from the machine:

1 insert the card into the slot

2 enter the PIN (personal identification number)

3 choose the service required (cash, cheque balance, request statement, etc)

4 select the amount of cash required

5 take back the card

6 take the money

7 take the receipt (if requested).

(When these machines were first installed, points 5 and 6 in the procedure above were reversed. This led to people forgetting to take their cards.)

Plastic cards

The card used to withdraw cash is a plastic card with a magnetic stripe (similar to ACCESS, VISA and MasterCard). The magnetic stripe holds about 72 characters and is coded with the following data:

- the card holder's account number
- their Personal Identification Number (PIN) – encoded on the card to stop fraud
- the sort code
- the card holder's withdrawal limit
- the amount withdrawn so far that day.

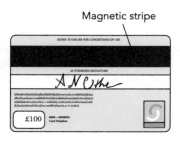

Magnetic stripe

Electronic Funds Transfer (EFT)

When a cash dispenser is used, the amount of money withdrawn is removed from the user's account. This movement of money electronically is referred to as an Electronic Funds Transfer. When paying for shopping in a supermarket using 'plastic' such as a Switch card, the payment is transferred electronically from the customer's account to the shop's account. The computerised till is known as a Point of Sale (POS) terminal. This transfer of funds is therefore called EFTPOS (Electronic Funds Transfer Point of Sale).

Computers in manufacturing

The car manufacturing industry was one of the first to use computer-controlled robots in the construction of vehicles. Since that time their use has become widespread across all sections of manufacturing. In order to increase productivity and decrease costs, manufacturers have found it necessary to replace workers with machines.

Although the initial cost of installing these computer-controlled machines is high, the low running costs quickly pay for the investment by decreasing labour costs. The advantages include:

- continuous operation, 24 hours per day, without tiring or tea breaks
- faster operations: a robotic arm can average one weld per second
- consistent and accurate work
- the ability to handle heavy loads
- the ability to work in hostile environments.

The diagram below illustrates some of the benefits:

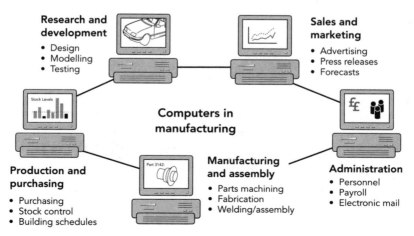

Research and development
- Design
- Modelling
- Testing

Sales and marketing
- Advertising
- Press releases
- Forecasts

Computers in manufacturing

Production and purchasing
- Purchasing
- Stock control
- Building schedules

Manufacturing and assembly
- Parts machining
- Fabrication
- Welding/assembly

Administration
- Personnel
- Payroll
- Electronic mail

Computers in other applications

Police Force: The Police National Computer (PNC) consists of several mainframe computers holding important files which help the police force in their investigation work. There are data files for cars containing information on the registration number, make, model and colour, and the owners details. There are data files for suspects, criminals, wanted and missing persons. There are files holding fingerprint and DNA data that allow police officers to search and match evidence at the scene of a crime with possible suspects.

Hospitals: The patients' records in a hospital are often kept on computer files. This allows data to be retrieved rapidly and transmitted electronically to different hospitals or surgeries. As patients dates of birth are held on file, it is a straightforward procedure to use the mailmerge facility of the computer software to send out reminder letters for inoculations. Computer equipment is used in intensive care wards to monitor patients, with heartbeat, temperature, pressure, and movement sensors inputting critical data from the patient. Databases are held with details of patients requiring transplant surgery. In the event of transplant organs becoming available, these can be matched quickly to an appropriate patient.

Questions

1   Two benefits to shop managers of using point-of-sale machines at supermarket checkouts are.

   a   managers can locate customers in the store at any time

   b   customers pass through the checkouts more quickly and with less errors being made

   c   it is easier to put the shopping into bags

   d   an itemised receipt describes the purchase and shows the price

   e   stock levels are adjusted automatically as the goods are scanned at the checkout.

2   There are only three sets of magnetic ink numbers on a bank cheque before it has been used. What do these numbers represent?

   a   ....

   b   ....

   c   ....

18 Effects of IT on society

As young people at school you are used to having computers around. You may have a computer at home to play games on or to help you with your school work. You will certainly use computers in your lessons at school. If you look around, you will see computers used in shops or your parents' workplaces, and you will often hear computers talked about on television.

Growth of computing

If you have chance to visit the computing section at the Science Museum you will see how very recent the development of computers has been. Engines, cars and motorcycles were invented over a hundred years ago and in comparison to computer development they have changed very little.

The first electronic computers, using glass tubes called valves, were constructed around 50 years ago. These first computers were used to calculate firing tables for field guns and to crack German codes during the war. Their processing power was very small by today's standards and the machines filled large rooms and consumed enormous quantities of power. The widespread use of computers in homes, schools and businesses only began about 20 years ago. Even today this growth continues; month by month computers become more sophisticated, have larger memories, better displays, faster processing, new features and yet the price remains the same or even falls.

Effect on society

This new age of computers is having an enormous impact on our lives. Some people wish it had never happened and long for the 'good old days', before computers, when the pace of life was much slower and less complicated. Others are greatly attracted by the opportunities this new technology offers. Life as we know it today, however, could not exist if this modern technology were removed. Without the aid of computerised technology we could not handle all the cheques written every day and the millions of telephone calls made. Even if all the unemployed people in the country were brought in to assist it would not be possible. Our standard of living would fall, prices would rise and on an international scale, any country that adopted this approach would be bound to fail in the competitive world in which we live.

Communication around the world has become almost instantaneous. For the price of a local telephone call, one can send messages around the globe by email. Huge quantities of information are available through the Internet and new skills are required to select and filter information needed from the various sources and articles. Information Technology allows documents to be faxed from one side of the world to the other. Information Technology is also responsible for the advances in satellite and cable television.

Communication through email and the access to information through the Internet is having a dramatic impact on our lives. Many more people are now working from home and this is set to increase as cameras mounted above monitors allow visual contact with other users. One possibility for future development is that all computers will have a radio link to the Internet, using similar technology to mobile phones.

It was once said that the use of computers would lead to the paperless office. In fact, computers generate far more paper than we had before. The amount of computerised mail that is delivered to our houses (bills, forms, advertising leaflets) shows that there is a lot of information about people held on computer files. Some data held on computers is highly confidential, for example, medical, financial and criminal data, and some of this data will be incorrect due to errors in the data sourcing and entry. These are issues that may affect our lives.

Effect on jobs

The introduction of computers has resulted in the loss of many jobs. In the early days, many of the jobs lost were those of unskilled workers whose repetitive tasks were replaced by machine. More recently computerisation has replaced jobs across most sections of the workplace. Even middle managers who make complex decisions using well-structured procedures have found that computer programs can replace them at a lower cost to the company.

The majority of jobs have been lost from the manufacturing industries but there has been an increase in jobs in the service sector; shops, hotels, catering and leisure industries. Part of this is due to the increased wealth generated by the more technologically advanced industries and also the increased leisure time available to workers. Many new jobs have been created in the IT and computing area, both in the manufacturing and service industries.

If a manufacturing plant invests in computerised equipment to replace its workers, then it will become more competitive as productivity rises and labour costs are reduced. However, some of its workers may be made redundant. If it does not computerise, the high labour costs and lower productivity result in the goods becoming less competitive and so the company starts to fail and all the workers lose their jobs. In addition, the nation loses the ability to manufacture those goods at a standard comparable to other countries. This illustrates the dilemma faced by employers, trade unions and governments.

Many people have had to retrain in new areas of work as computerised systems have replaced their original jobs. It is necessary in society today to have a flexible workforce where individuals may have to retrain for employment two or three times during their working lives. It is also important for individuals to understand how computers work and the effects that Information Technology has on their lives so that they can influence the changes that are taking place and ensure a better quality of life results from those changes.

Questions

1   Information Technology makes it easier for people to work from home. Describe one advantage and one disadvantage of home working.

....

....

....

....

....

....

2   Describe how the increased use of IT for home shopping and banking may affect changes in society.

....

....

....

....

....

....

....

19 Data protection

The Data Protection Act

The 'right to privacy' is a right we all expect. We do not expect our personal details such as our age, medical records, personal family details, politics and religious beliefs to be freely available to everybody. With the growth of Information Technology, large databases are able to hold huge quantities of information and global networks are able to share and distribute this information around the world in seconds. In order to control this development and to protect people's right to privacy the Data Protection Act became law in July 1984.

If any person, organisation, company or business wishes to hold personal information about people on a database then this must be registered with the Data Protection Registrar's office. A fee must be paid and forms completed to show:

- your details (name and address)
- details of the data you wish to hold about people together with the reason for holding it
- details of the source of the data
- details of any people to whom you may disclose the data.

The Data Protection Act contains eight basic principles, as shown below:

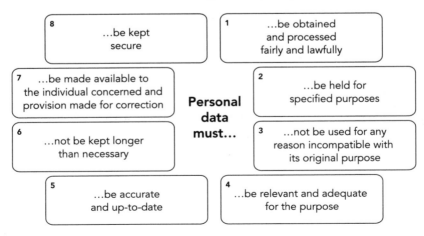

8 ...be kept secure	**1** ...be obtained and processed fairly and lawfully
7 ...be made available to the individual concerned and provision made for correction	**2** ...be held for specified purposes
6 ...not be kept longer than necessary	**3** ...not be used for any reason incompatible with its original purpose
5 ...be accurate and up-to-date	**4** ...be relevant and adequate for the purpose

Personal data must...

There are certain exemptions to the Act and the rules governing the need to register a computer database. These are:

- data that is related to national security
- data that is required by law to be made public
- data that is only concerned with personal and family affairs
- some data relating to the accounts of a business including salaries, wages and pensions
- data relating to crime detection
- data relating to immigration
- data relating to income tax assessment and collection
- data not held on computer.

The Data Protection Act attempts to offer protection to individuals against information that is inaccurate. You will see from the list of exceptions that there is no similar protection offered to individuals where data is held on paper in filing cabinets.

Looking after computer data

In business the data stored in a computer can be hundreds of times more valuable than the actual computer equipment. This data may include all the company's financial records, all its customers' details, records of the stock held, etc. Losing this data could, in some cases, put companies out of business.

Data can be damaged or destroyed in the following ways:

- breakdown of hardware, particularly disk drives
- mistakes by office staff, eg deleting files
- poor office practice, eg not taking a regular back-up of data files and not checking for viruses
- hackers gaining access to systems and changing/deleting data
- computer fraud where data is changed to benefit individuals
- theft of computer equipment
- fire, floods, hurricanes, earthquakes, etc, destroying equipment
- infection of systems and data by computer viruses
- deliberate and malicious damage by staff.

Back-ups

Taking a back-up of the data from the hard disk drive of a computer or from the hard disk of a file server running a network is vital. One certain fact is that a hard disk drive will not run forever. If a back-up is taken at the end of each day, then the most that can be lost is one day's work. Often special tape drive units are used to back-up the data from a disk drive. A number of tapes should be used in rotation so that a back-up copy can always be kept away from the premises.

Data is backed up onto tape and then put in a safe place

These tape back-ups should be kept away from the original data, in another building or on another site. Sometimes smaller business encourage office staff to take back-up tapes home with them so that data will not be lost through theft from the offices. Tapes kept on-site should be deposited safely each evening in a fireproof safe.

Hackers

A hacker is a person who breaks codes and passwords to gain unauthorised entry to computer systems. Hackers can do an enormous amount of damage if they break into a computer system. For some people the challenge of breaking the codes is irresistible and so precautions have to be taken. 'Stand-alone' computers are usually safe as there is no connection for the hackers to break into. Computers which form part of networks or those with external links, such as attached modems, are in danger from hackers. It is necessary to use passwords to log on to the computer system and it is important to change these passwords at regular intervals.

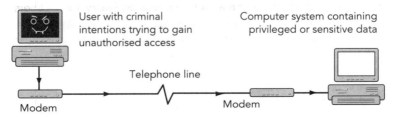

Computers connected to networks or modems are at risk from hacking

Computer fraud

Computer fraud is a criminal activity where computer operators use the computer to their own advantage. It is thought that only one in ten cases of computer fraud are reported. There are a number of reasons for this:

- it is very hard to track down and the people committing the crime are often very clever
- offenders are often young, with no previous criminal records
- when fraud is discovered in a company it is often not publicised as news of the fraud may damage the image of the company.

One example of computer fraud involved a computer operator who found a blank payroll form. He completed the form, making up the details for an imaginary person working in the company. Each month, as the pay cheques were produced from the company computer, he was able to slip the cheque into his pocket without anyone realising.

Computer viruses

In the same way that human viruses use the human body's own system to reproduce themselves, so computer viruses are small programs that 'hijack' a computer and use it to reproduce and spread themselves.

How viruses spread

There are hundreds of different viruses and more are being created every month by people intent on damaging other people's computer systems. The viruses attach themselves to computer programs and data files. They then spread by copying themselves onto floppy disks, then onto other hard disks and also across networks – all without the knowledge of the user. It is quite possible to connect to the Internet, download an email message and gain a virus in the process.

How they are activated

Viruses are activated in different ways. Some are activated by the internal clock and will start running on a particular day, eg Friday 13th. Others activate when a series of conditions are true, eg when a certain combination of keys are pressed on the keyboard. Virus programs generally destroy and corrupt data on the computer's hard disk.

Removing viruses

There are a number of anti-virus programs available for wiping out viruses but with any anti-virus program it is important to have regular updates to deal with the new viruses. When the anti-virus software is run it scans the hard disk looking for virus patterns. This software cleans the virus off the disk and alerts the user to the damage caused by the virus.

The Computer Misuse Act, 1990

Hacking, computer fraud and computer virus are all relatively new crimes that established English laws were not designed to deal with. For example, under existing laws a hacker could only be prosecuted for the theft of electricity. To deal with these new crimes a law was introduced in 1990 called The Compute Misuse Act. Under this law, the following offences could be dealt with:

- Hacking – unauthorised access to any program or data held in a computer.

  Fine (maximum £2000) and prison sentence (maximum 6 months)

- Computer Fraud and Blackmail

  Fine (maximum unlimited) and prison sentence (maximum 5 years)

- Viruses – unauthorised modification of the contents of a computer, impairing the operation of any program or reliability of data.

  Fine (maximum unlimited) and prison sentence (maximum 5 years)

The Copyright, Designs and Patents Act, 1989

Copying computer software, or software piracy, is now a criminal offence under this 1989 Act. The Act covers stealing software, using illegally copied software and manuals, and running purchased software on two or more machines at the same time without a suitable licence. Quite often organisations will purchase software licences to cover the number of stations on their network. They then neglect to purchase additional software licences as they buy more workstations.

The legal penalties for breaking the copyright law include unlimited fines and up to two years in prison.

It has been estimated that half the software used is copied illegally and in some countries pirated software accounts for 90% of the total. Two organisations fight to stop software being copied:

- FAST (Federation Against Software Theft) – founded in 1984, a non-profit organisation to promote the legal use of software.

- BSA (Business Software Alliance) – exist to make organisations and their employees aware of the law and encourage its implementation.

Questions

1 Two of the statements shown below are a summary of the eight principles set out in the Data Protection Act 1984. Which two are they?

   a ☐   Personal data may not be made available to the individual concerned and provision made for correction.

   b ☐   Data must not be used for purposes other than those originally intended and the holder has a duty to protect the data.

   c ☐   Those organisations that are exempt from the Data Protection Act do not need to register with the Data Protection Registrar's office but they are required by law to follow the principles of the Act.

   d ☐   The right for individuals to know what data is being held and to be able to correct it.

2 Gaining access to computers illegally can cause serious problems. Describe two problems it can cause and two ways of preventing it from happening.

   ....

   ....

3 Explain the term computer virus, and give two precautions which should be taken to avoid a computer virus affecting a computer.

   ....

   ....

   ....

4 Describe two different situations when it might be necessary to use the back-up copies taken from a hard disk drive.

   ....

   ....

5 Which of the following is not exempt from the Data Protection Act? Data held:

   a ☐   for national security

   b ☐   to prevent crime

   c ☐   by a company for direct mail

   d ☐   for tax purposes?

Answers

Input devices (page 12)

1 CD-ROM – used a source of clipart pictures; Scanner – to input photographs
2 Country of origin
3 The price of the product may need to change
4 a Thermistor (temperature sensor) or light-dependent resistor (light sensor)
  b Concept keyboard
  c Optical character recognition
  d Optical mark recognition
  e Magnetic stripe on a debit/credit card

Output devices (page 19)

1 Input – push button switches
  Output – LCD display
2 Plotter
3 a Laser printer
  b Ink-jet
  c Dot-matrix
4 a For blind users
  b Flat-bed plotters, robotic arms
  c Digital watches, calculators
5 a Speed
  b High resolution graphics

Computer memory (page 21)

Words in correct order are: megabytes, RAM, memory, eight

Backing store (page 24)

1 a Less possibility of damaging or corrupting programs and data, stores much more data, better graphics and sound, more difficult to produce illegal copies, CD used when playing the game so no need to use up valuable hard disk drive space
  b Not all home computers have CD drives, not all games are produced on CD as well as floppy disks
2 To transfer programs and data between computers, to keep back-ups of data, to store programs and data in a safe location

Operating systems (page 27)

1 Words in correct order are: multiprocessor, multiuser/multitasking, realtime, batch
2 d Printing a telephone directory

Human–computer interface (page 29)

1 a The movement of the mouse to control the screen pointer, mouse buttons to select, drag and activate menu options
  b Use of drop-down menus, selection of menu choice by clicking mouse buttons, use of icons, dragging over text to highlight, etc

2 Another action is required first, eg you cannot choose 'Edit ... paste' until a picture or text has been selected and 'Edit ... copy or cut' has occurred

Databases (pages 51 and 52)

1 a and b
2 Customer name, address, customer number, telephone, account number, account balance
3 Words in correct order are: customer, file, fields, unique, key
4 a GEO2FLO
  b ART1EMC
  c Less space/memory used, faster processing, fixed length fields
5 a Book information
  b Large capacity for data, sound and moving pictures
  c Data can be altered – records added, edited and deleted
6 Range check, >0 and <13

Spreadsheets (page 59)

a =sum(D3:D6) or D3+D4+D5+D6
b i Text (cells in row 1 or column A or C8)
  ii Numbers (cells B3-B6 or C3-C6)
c Alter values in column C until required total value reached
d Words in correct order are: formatted, formula, copied, D5, D8

CAD/CAM (page 63)

1 Computer Aided Design
2 Zooming, rotation, enlargement, boxes, circles, infill, shading, colours, save, load, plot, text, dimensions, scaling
3 Two from: Bigger screen (typically 20 inches+), much higher resolution, more expensive

CD-ROMs and multimedia (page 67)

Two from: Music, speech, video, animations, photographs, graphics

Data logging (page 71)

a Light-dependent resistor (LDR)
b Analogue
c Digital
d The substances are likely to react too quickly for measurements to be taken by hand, data logging equipment takes measurements with high speed and accuracy
e The light sensor would be replaced by a thermistor input device positioned in the liquid. The light would be removed as this would act as an additional heat source

Computer control (pages 79 and 80)

1 a Total_cars = cars_start + cars_in − cars_out
   b If total_cars<max_cars
   c Use a pressure sensor which will respond to the weight of a car but not people
   d If car park full, how long the queue is. How quickly are cars coming in and out. Estimates of how many spaces may be available in the next 15 mins, 30 mins, 45 mins, etc based on spaces available now and data from recent days/weeks – this will give useful information to someone who may take half an hour to reach town

2 a Package 3 F3,2; Package 4 B1,2; Package 5 F2,3
   b Equip the forklift truck with sensors to read positional data in the warehouse, eg markings on the floor

Communication (pages 87 and 88)

1 a This will stop unauthorised users from logging onto the network or accessing files in another user's directory
   b A password may be seen by another user so their data will no longer be secure
   c Password is being verified to ensure that a wrong key was not pressed when the new password was typed in

2 Words in correct order are: LAN, modem, WAN, email

3 a Star topology
   b The vets can access their data files from any of the surgeries' programs can be shared, easier to back-up the data (just the file server to back-up, not every machine)
   c Modem
   d Converts the digital signals from the computer to sound signals (analogue) so data can be sent along telephone lines
   e Unauthorised users may hack into the computer using the telephone lines and modem. They could corrupt data, introduce viruses and gain access to confidential data

File structures (page 91)

1 With random (direct) access the disk drive head can move directly to the data on the disk using the address. In serial access it is necessary to start at the beginning of the file and read in, one by one, until the required data is found

2 a 24/1200 x 100 = 2%
   b 900/1200 x 100 = 75%

System design and development (page 100)

System requirements, program installation notes, instructions on how to use the program, examples of the different screens, troubleshooting guide (ie how to deal with errors)

Applications of IT (page 106)

1 b and e
2 a Cheque number
   b Bank sort code
   c Account number

Effects of IT on society (page 109)

1 Advantages: Flexible working hours, time and money not spent commuting to work, reduced costs for expensive office space, more comfortable working environment
   Disadvantages: Less interaction with colleagues generating new ideas, possible feeling of isolation, expensive telephone bills through communicating with others

2 Less interaction between people, less staff needed in shops and less traffic on the roads, reduced need to locate shops in expensive town and city centres, potential increase in crime using IT

Data protection (page 115)

1 b and d
2 Problems caused: The data may be confidential, it could be passed to business competitors, data could be changed
   Preventing: Restrict access to the computer, ensure supervisor monitors computer use, use passwords, message should be relayed to computer manager after several incorrect password attempts, encrypt data

3 A virus is a computer program designed to damage or destroy computer programs and data in the computer. A virus can duplicate itself by passing to computer hard disks from floppy disks or across networks. Precautions: Check disks for viruses using anti-virus software, don't use outside disks on the computer

4 System crash causing damage to the data on the disk, equipment stolen and data needs reinstalling on new equipment, important files deleted accidentally and need to be recovered, hackers change data

5 c – by a company for direct mail

Index

Tt

Uu

Vv

Ww